Patrick Kavanagh

PATRICK KAVANAGH

By JOHN NEMO

Bradley University

TWAYNE PUBLISHERS
A Division of G. K. Hall & Co.
Boston, Massachusetts, U. S. A.

Frontispiece photograph
of Patrick Kavanagh
courtesy of MacGibbon and Kee Publishers

Library of Congress Cataloging in Publication Data

Nemo, John.
Patrick Kavanagh.

(Twayne's English authors series ; TEAS 267)
Bibliography: p. 155 - 61
Includes index.
1.   Kavanagh, Patrick, 1904 - 1967
—Criticism and interpretation.
PR6021.A74Z79   821'.9'12   79-11031
ISBN 0-8057-6770-3

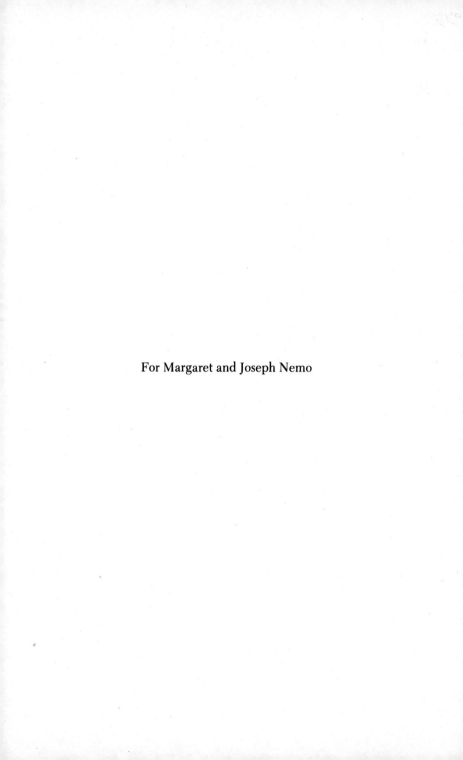

For Margaret and Joseph Nemo

Contents

About the Author

Born and raised in St. Paul, Minnesota, John Nemo was educated at St. Thomas College (B.A.), Southern Illinois University (M.A.), and The National University of Ireland (Ph.D.). He presently teaches modern poetry and fiction at Bradley University, where he also serves as Director of Graduate Studies in English.

Professor Nemo has published essays and articles on Irish literature in such journals as *Studies*, *The Journal of Irish Literature*, and the *Irish University Review*. In addition to editing P. J. O'Connor's adaptation of *Tarry Flynn* for The New Abbey Theatre Series, Dr. Nemo edited the special number of *The Journal of Irish Literature* devoted to Patrick Kavanagh.

Married and the father of two daughters and a son, Professor Nemo and his wife Patricia live in Peoria, Illinois.

Preface

The general aim of this book is to introduce readers to the work of the Irish poet Patrick Kavanagh, an important contemporary writer who has been misunderstood and neglected. Hailed in various literary circles as the best Irish poet since the death of William Butler Yeats, Kavanagh has yet to achieve either popular or critical acclaim outside the borders of his native Ireland. This is unfortunate, for in both his fiction and poetry he has made important contributions to modern literature. *Tarry Flynn*, for example, a semiautobiographical novel about rural life, is both an entertaining and authentic portrait of the Irish countryside. This book, like the best of Kavanagh's writing, demonstrates his talent for portraying the common man's daily triumphs and tragedies without sinking into either sentimentality or didacticism. Another of Kavanagh's achievements is reflected in his capacity to treat human problems in an Irish setting without reverting to the trite divisions of squire and peasant, a weakness typical of many Irish writers.

Kavanagh's most significant achievement is his long poem, *The Great Hunger*, one of the finest statements of the rigor, the humor, and the horror of Irish peasant life. Aside from its other aspects, *The Great Hunger* is particularly important because it plumbs an Irish landscape to articulate universal themes without losing the texture of the Irish scene. This poem more than any other work clearly illustrates that Kavanagh, unlike certain other Irish writers, is no mere local colorist. In both his early and later work Kavanagh was able to use Irish locality as subject matter and metaphor, an achievement which has become an important influence on the development of a number of more recent Irish writers. Because *The Great Hunger* makes such a striking and successful use of Irish locality as subject matter and metaphor, one of Ireland's leading publishers has hailed it as "the watershed" of contemporary Irish poetry.

It is unfortunate that Kavanagh's work is so little known in America. It is even more unfortunate that in Ireland and England, where his work has received some attention, there is a curious tendency to confuse his life-style with his poetry. Too often his admirers blindly affirm his poetic achievement because they still savor his unconventional and often outrageous social habits, while his detractors, those who have been savaged by either his pen or his tongue, dismiss him as an undisciplined and ill-tempered peasant. Even those who attempt some middle ground tend to view him as some sort of holy fool. In light of this, there is a real need for an objective, critical examination of Kavanagh's writing so that his accomplishments and his importance to modern poetry may be clarified.

To provide a context for this study, the book begins with a biographical statement, then presents four chapters which detail the various phases of Kavanagh's poetic career. The final chapter examines the nature of his literary success and evaluates his contribution to contemporary Irish poetry.

Because there are numerous textual errors in *Collected Poems, Complete Poems, Collected Pruse,* and *November Haggard,* citations from Kavanagh's literary works have been taken from either first publications or republications authorized by Kavanagh himself.

Peoria, Illinois

Acknowledgments

I am indebted to many people. Professor Roger McHugh, University College Dublin, offered advice, information, and sound critical guidance. Poet and Professor Thomas Kinsella, Temple University, not only introduced me to the work of Patrick Kavanagh, but also calmed troubled waters on numerous occasions. Others who contributed in a variety of ways include: Adrian Cronin, Joan and Brian Conroy, Bill Doyle, Peter Dusenbery, Maureen and Peter Kenny, Benedict Kiely, Augustine Martin, Peadar O'Donnell, Sean O'Faolain, Patrick O'Keefe, John Ryan, Bella and John Scott, Michael Scott, Niall Sheridan, and Alan Warner. A special thanks to Professors Dennis McInerny and David Pichaske, colleagues of mine at Bradley University, and to the Bradley University Board for Research and Creative Production for research funds. Finally, it would have been impossible to write this book without the aid, understanding, and advice of Jennifer, Clare, John Michael, and, most significantly, my wife Patricia.

For the opportunity to quote from Patrick Kavanagh's published and unpublished works I would like to thank the *Irish Farmers' Journal*, the *Irish Independent*, the *Irish Times*, *The Irish Press*, The National Library of Ireland, the Kavanagh Estate, and Martin, Brian & O'Keeffe, Ltd.

Chronology

1904   Born October 21 at Inniskeen, County Monaghan, to James and Bridget Kavanagh.

1916   Leaves Kednaminsha Grammar School, begins writing juvenile verse.

1923   Contracts typhoid fever from drinking water out of a stream near family farm, spends three months in Fever Hospital in Carrickmacross, returns home with permanent thrombosis in the leg.

1925   Elected captain of local Tug O' War team.

1926   Purchase of Reynolds Farm by James Kavanagh for his son Patrick.

1927   Frequents Dundalk library and bookshops.

1928   Publishes "An Address to an Old Wooden Gate" in *Dundalk Democrat* and "The Intangible" in the *Irish Statesman*. Father dies August 27.

1930   Walks to Dublin to meet AE (George Russell). Tours Connemara. Meets Seumas O'Sullivan, editor of *The Dublin Magazine*.

1931   Publishes "Beech Tree" and other poems in *The Dublin Magazine*.

1932   Elected captain-treasurer of Rovers, local football club.

1933   Frequents Dublin; meets Frank O'Connor and Sean O'Faolain.

1935   Attends AE's funeral in Dublin.

1936   *Ploughman and Other Poems* published by Macmillan, Ltd. as a number of the "Contemporary Poets Series." "Listen" and "The Hired Boy" published in *Ireland Today*.

1937   Travels to London in June and meets Sean O'Casey, G. B. Shaw, the poet John Gawsworth, and other members of the London literary set. Writes *The Green Fool* and returns to Dublin.

1938   *The Green Fool* published by Michael Joseph, Ltd. "Fool" and "The Irony of It" in the *Irish Times*. Delivers broad-

	cast, "I Hate That Book," on Radio Eireann and presents short program on BBC Northern Ireland.
1939	Awarded AE Memorial Prize (£100) for published and proposed work.
1940	Begins career in journalism with occasional articles and semi-regular book reviews for the *Irish Times*.
1942	"The Old Peasant" (first stanzas of *The Great Hunger*) published in *Horizon*, with the result that the magazine is removed from circulation and two Dublin detectives visit Kavanagh at his flat. *The Great Hunger* published by The Cuala Hand Press.
1943	Moves to 62 Pembroke Road, his Dublin residence until 1955. Begins "City Commentary" in *The Irish Press*.
1945	"Fifty Years Achievement" published in *The Standard*. Bridget Quinn Kavanagh (mother) dies at age 73.
1946	Joins *The Standard* as subeditor and cinema critic. Holds these jobs until 1949.
1947	Macmillan issues *A Soul for Sale* in February. Several extracts from *Tarry Flynn* published in *The Bell*. Cancels proposed visit to United States when offered £600 advance from Macmillan to remain in Ireland as a creative writer—contract to run through 1949.
1948	"Poetry in Ireland Today" appears in *The Bell*. *Tarry Flynn* published by The Pilot Press in London and banned by the Irish Censorship Board. Steady reviewing for *The Irish Press* and the *Irish Times*.
1949	Sells Reynolds Farm for £450. "The Paddiad" in August number of *Horizon*. Loses advance from Macmillan because of contract with The Pilot Press. Monthly "Diary" begins in *Envoy*.
1950	Works on new novel. Continues to publish "Diary" in *Envoy*. Spends summer in London looking for work and travels to Rome in October.
1951	Offered the position of British Isles Advisor by Seven Sirens Press. Spends winter in London and presents talk on BBC Third Program. "Three Pieces from a Novel" in *The Bell*.
1952	Writes, edits, and publishes *Kavanagh's Weekly* from April 12 to July 5. October 11 *The Leader* "Profile" appears and Kavanagh returns from London to Dublin to start libel proceedings.
1953	Presses for Court action against *The Leader*. "A Goat

Tethered Outside the Bailey" featured in *The Bell*. Suffers a severe case of alcoholic poisoning in November.

1954   February 3, libel suit against *The Leader* begins. Verdict of "not guilty" returned February 12. Kavanagh takes job as spray-painting salesman (May through July). Organizes appeal; heard November 16 to 26. Judgment is "reserved." December, receives letter from John Costello, Taoiseach, assuring him a job in the near future.

1955   Granted opportunity to re-present case against *The Leader*. Enters Rialto Hospital (March 1) with cancer of the lung. After lung is removed, makes dramatic recovery. Spends spring in Longford, summer in Dublin. Announces his rebirth on the banks of the Grand Canal. Awarded £400 yearly sinecure through the efforts of John Costello.

1957   February, begins series of ten extramural lectures at University College Dublin. Spends July on French Riviera with American friends. Begins new monthly column in *Creation*, a Dublin fashion magazine.

1958   Begins weekly column in *Irish Farmers' Journal* (continues to appear through March, 1963). *Recent Poems* published by Peter Kavanagh Hand Press (limited to 25 numbered copies signed by author). Delivers four extramural lectures at University College Dublin.

1960   *Come Dance with Kitty Stobling and Other Poems* published by Macmillan in March and selected as a choice of the Poetry Society. Introduces a reading of *The Great Hunger* on BBC Third Program. Selected for a second time to be judge for the Guinness Poetry Competition. Contracts with Hutchinson, Ltd. to write autobiography. Health begins to fail.

1961   Delivers eight extramural lectures at University College Dublin. Receives commission from Guinness to write "The Gambler." Continues to suffer poor health. Receives contract from MacGibbon & Kee, Ltd. to publish *Collected Poems*. Four Square Books advance £150 toward reprinting *Tarry Flynn*. Enters Baggot Street hospital in December with bronchial pneumonia and gastritis.

1963   Writes in an unposted letter: "since 1950 I have changed in some respects; I no longer think it necessary to make fierce attacks on foolish poets and storytellers." Presents *Self Portrait* on Telefis Eireann.

1964   Suffering from kidney trouble and osteoarthritis, he writes "Preface" for *Collected Poems*. Begins weekly column in *RTV Guide*.

1965   Visits New York and Chicago. Gathers materials for *Collected Pruse*.

1966   *Tarry Flynn* is produced at the Abbey Theatre (for a four-week run). Presents program about County Monaghan for Telefis Eireann.

1967   Spends winter in Inniskeen, very ill. April, marries Katherine Maloney in Dublin. *Collected Pruse* published by MacGibbon & Kee, Ltd. Writes preface to *The Autobiography of William Carleton*. Dies November 30.

CHAPTER 1

From Monaghan to the Grand Canal

PATRICK Kavanagh is one of the most controversial Irish writers of the post-Celtic Revival period. Though he died in 1967, his presence is still very much alive in Irish literary circles. His followers, a varied but vocal group, speak of him admiringly as an important force in Irish letters, second only to William Butler Yeats. His detractors, fewer but every bit as vocal, dismiss him as a loud-mouthed, ill-mannered peasant who disrupted rather than advanced the development of modern literature. Between these two groups are those readers who acknowledge and praise his genuine poetic gift yet recognize his occasionally outrageous and sometimes contradictory pronouncements about writing, his contemporaries, and Ireland. Despite this diversity of opinion, there is no denying that Kavanagh has had, for good or ill, a significant impact on recent Irish literature. There is also no denying that Kavanagh was and is a celebrated Dublin character. And it is primarily from this duality of presence that the controversy surrounding the man continues to sustain itself. In short, many of Kavanagh's commentators, friend and foe alike, give in to the temptation to judge Kavanagh the character rather than Kavanagh the poet in their evaluations. To appreciate his role in contemporary Irish literature, or to assess his critical and creative achievement, then, requires a clarification of the relationship between his life and work.

I Literary Beginnings

Patrick Joseph Kavanagh was born at 8:45 PM on Sunday, October 21, 1904—not 1905, the date usually given. He was the fourth child (and first son) born to James and Bridget Kavanagh in the Townland of Mucker, Inniskeen Parish, County Monaghan. In most ways Kavanagh's youth was typical of the time and place in which he grew into young manhood. The most complete account of these

years is contained in *The Green Fool*, his earliest attempt at
autobiography. Aside from the fact that certain parts of the book
suffer from Kavanagh's admission of having little memory for
anything save the quaint and the bizarre, many of the details he
relates are true. He began to write juvenile verse, for example,
sometime after his twelfth birthday. Though most of these early
attempts at poetry are lost, such verses as "Farrelly Climbed in the
Window," "The Band Turned Out," and "The Shoemaker" have
survived and are included in *Lapped Furrows*. Not surprisingly,
these first poetic efforts all feature the usual forced rhymes and
singsong rhythms characteristic of schoolboy poetry. Beneath their
overly sentimental tone, however, are elements of the comic vision
that was to become one of Kavanagh's literary strengths.

During the years when he wrote his notebook verse, Kavanagh's
relationship with his family and his growing interest in literature
combined to make him feel an outsider in his native community.
This predilection for seeing himself apart from his family and —
later in his life — society as a whole, was constant from his
childhood to his last days in Dublin and is reflected in much of his
writing, from his sense of personal fault in the early poetry to his
declaration of failure in *Self Portrait*. While he treats this aspect of
his personality with humor in *The Green Fool* — the very title of
the books suggests his concern, however — *Tarry Flynn* is the most
sustained and perhaps the most serious attempt to explain this facet
of his personality. This sense of being different, of being on the outside, as it were, had several lasting effects on him. It served to support his idea of artistic distance when he began to feel a growing interest in literature during his late teens and early twenties. All of his
life he enjoyed reflecting on and talking about the presence of the
poet that he felt in himself. He goes to great pains in *Tarry Flynn*,
for example, to point out Tarry's awareness of the "kink" in himself
that set him apart from his family and neighbors. It is the same sen-
sation that Kavanagh writes about in his preface to *Collected Poems*
when he says that poetry made him an outcast.

It was essentially because of this sense of artistic isolation that
Kavanagh attempted to join what he believed in the late 1930s was
an important circle of Irish artists who were living in Dublin. When
his initial acceptance into this group failed to mature past his reception as the peasant poet, he turned on these writers and condemned
them as pseudo-artists, declaring in *Self Portrait* that their conversation was nothing more than "tiresome drivel between journalists
and civil servants."[1]

II *Literary Apprenticeship*

Kavanagh served his literary apprenticeship during the years 1928 - 1936. His basic texts were the works of Percy Shelley, John Keats, Alexander Pope, John Milton, and numerous other literary masters whose works he borrowed from friends or from the Dundalk library. He supplemented these classics with the contemporary poetry and fiction he found in magazines like *Poetry*, *The Dublin Magazine*, and the *Irish Statesman*. To learn technique he copied popular songs into his notebooks and studied their rhyme and rhythm patterns. He also had access to a copy of *Intermediate Poetry and Prose*, a schoolbook belonging to one of his sisters which dealt in part with the craft of poetry. With these books to direct him and serve as examples to be imitated, Kavanagh spent many evenings writing poems about himself and his life on the farm.

In August, 1928, he entered three of his efforts in a weekly competition, "Poet's Corner," sponsored by the *Irish Weekly Independent*. His poem "Freedom" placed second and was published on September 1, 1928. During the next ten months he published fourteen poems in this newspaper.[2] In the autumn of 1929 he sent several poems to the *Irish Statesman*. Although they were rejected, he was told by the editor, AE (George Russell), to submit more material. The publication of "The Intangible," "Ploughman," and "Dreamer" in the *Irish Statesman* in 1929 - 1930 signalled Kavanagh's arrival as more than a "Poet's Corner" artist. His literary fortunes were furthered too by the correspondence he exchanged with AE, who not only offered a paying market for poetry but also served briefly as a mentor, suggesting ways of improving Kavanagh's writing. By the autumn of 1930 the desire to venture away from the farm had grown too strong for Kavanagh to resist. He decided to visit Dublin, using the closing of the *Irish Statesman* that previous April as his excuse. In a somewhat fictionalized account of this junket recorded in *The Green Fool* Kavanagh explains how he succeeded in meeting AE and Seamus O'Sullivan, then editor of *The Dublin Magazine*.[3]

In April, 1936, Kavanagh signed a contract with Macmillan for the publication of his first book, *Ploughman and Other Poems*. Issued during the summer, the collection sold for one shilling and was well received in England and Dublin, though it was ignored in Inniskeen and Dundalk. This book had several significant effects on Kavanagh's life and on the development of his poetry. It brought about, first of all, an immediate increase in his status and reputa-

tion. In particular, his image as a peasant poet was more or less per-
manently fixed by the positive critical reception the book received.
In a literary arena that had known only synthetic peasant
visionaries, Kavanagh was the genuine article. The manure on his
boots was real.

The book's reception also caused Kavanagh to question seriously
the value of residing in Inniskeen. He spent the winter of 1936 - 37
struggling with his dilemma. On the one hand, if he left his farm he
would be sacrificing the security that the land provided him, a fact
drummed into him over the years by his mother. He would have to
give up a way of life that was familiar and, in many ways, quite
pleasant. On the other hand, there were certain aspects of his life in
Inniskeen that he found dull and oppressive. The thought of being
tied to one place and one mode of existence for the rest of his days
frustrated him. Not only did he have a distaste for the more boring
tasks and duties he had as a cobbler-farmer, but he also feared the
effects of living among people insensitive to his perceptions. While
he believed that if he stayed in Inniskeen his talent might be stifled,
he also believed that the farm offered him the surest opportunity of
marriage and the pleasures of raising a family. As he thought about
his problem and tried to reason out what he should do, he received
little real aid from either his family or his friends. By spring,
however, he had made up his mind to leave Inniskeen temporarily
for London, not Dublin. Promising correspondence with several
London publishers was the factor that decided the issue.[4] In addition, Kavanagh hoped to find a job with one of the English
periodicals that had been buying his poetry. So in May of 1937 he
left the farm and travelled to England in hopes of finding his
literary fortune.

One year later his second book, *The Green Fool*, was published
by Michael Joseph in London. Unfortunately for Kavanagh, the
book's circulation was stopped by a lawsuit brought by Oliver St.
John Gogarty, who objected to a sketch in which Kavanagh claimed
to have mistaken Gogarty's "white-robed maid" for his wife or mistress, explaining that in his country naiveté he had expected every
poet to "have a spare wife."[5] Toward the end of his life Kavanagh
complained that this legal action hindered the development of his
talent. However, the fact that he wrote *The Great Hunger*, one of
the finest long poems of this century, within three years of *The
Green Fool* affair indicates his claim had little basis in fact.

Despite the lawsuit, *The Green Fool* received a number of

favorable reviews. One critic, Harold Nicolson, particularly praised it and heralded Kavanagh as a writer who could well become the Irish Robert Burns.[6] The book also corroborated the peasant poet image suggested by *Ploughman and Other Poems*. However, *The Green Fool* is a more mature book than *Ploughman*. Written in a relaxed, casual style, it presents a series of light-hearted and rather romantic recollections which trace Kavanagh's life from his early childhood days in Inniskeen to his arrival in London shortly before the coronation of George VI. In a later autobiography Kavanagh rejected *The Green Fool* as a stage-Irish lie, explaining that he wrote it "under the evil aegis of the so-called Irish Literary Movement."[7] No doubt much of the book is fabrication. No doubt, too, it was written to appeal to an audience who, conditioned by the Celtic Revival, had come to expect a certain degree of exaggeration from an Irish writer, particularly from one so close to the "ould sod." But the book is neither stage-Irishry nor a lie. Whatever its faults, its appearance demonstrated that Kavanagh had become a professional writer, skilled in his craft and capable of organizing and executing an informative and highly entertaining piece of writing.

III *Poet and Journalist*

After a year split between the farm and Dublin, Kavanagh moved himself on a more or less permanent basis to Dublin in 1939. It was a decision he was to ruminate over the rest of his life, particularly in the last six or seven years before he died. His bitterest remark about the event came in 1963 in *Self Portrait*:

It was the worst mistake of my life. The Hitler war had started. I had my comfortable little holding of watery hills beside the Border. What was to bate it for a life? And yet I wasted what could have been my four glorious years, begging and scrambling around the streets of malignant Dublin.[4]

Despite the sentiment here, Kavanagh knew in 1963 as he did in 1939 that he had had no real choice in the matter—which may have made his recollection all the more bitter. Nevertheless, he found himself in Dublin in 1939 trying to earn his living by his pen, and so began the fourteen-year period in which he made his name famous as a poet and infamous as a critic.

Shortly after his arrival in Dublin, Kavanagh associated with a circle of literati who either were or claimed to be poets, novelists,

and dramatists. Described by one of their number as a literary un-
derworld, and by another as a pack of gray wolves who sharpened
their critical teeth on the bones of each other's talent, this group
met in the Palace Bar, a popular "writers pub" of the day.[9] Cyril
Connelly, then editor of *Horizon*, once described the Palace as

a small back room in a tavern which is frequented entirely by writers and
journalists; it is as warm and friendly as an alligator tank, its inhabitants,
from a long process of mutual mastication, have a leathery look.[10]

The mean nature of the Palace Bar habitués was symptomatic of
a general depression which had settled over Ireland during these
years. This legacy from "The Troubles," that bitter period of
rebellion, civil war, and political strife from 1916 through the 1920s,
produced a society politically and culturally isolated from England
and Western Europe. Governmental policies reinforced the paralyzing insularism. In addition, the Catholic Church, always a conservative body in Ireland, was in certain ways more powerful than the
Irish government and exercised a stifling influence. Censorship and
other restrictive measures hindered the creative development of
Irish artists of all types.

Kavanagh became disenchanted with the Palace Bar and Dublin
in general. He found little worthwhile employment and was forced
to endure considerable financial hardship. He was also an outsider.
As a countryman he lacked the social graces, the education, and the
money he believed many of his literary colleagues enjoyed. He felt
discriminated against and isolated, and lashed out with rudeness
and bluster. But more important, Kavanagh was offended by the
lack of vitality and commitment to literature he found in Dublin.
The would-be writers who populated the Palace Bar talked rather
than wrote poetry or fiction. They were critics not creators. And
perhaps worst of all, from Kavanagh's point of view, their ideas
about the purpose and method of literature were radically different
from his own.

In this environment, from the late 1930s to the early 1950s,
Kavanagh pursued poetry and financed himself by writing three
serial columns, hundreds of signed and unsigned book reviews,
several dozen essays, articles and human interest stories, and, in
1952, thirteen issues of his own weekly newspaper. He turned out
this journal with zest. To draw attention to his writing, he
developed his own distinctive critical voice. Some readers thought it

was the voice of hysteria, while others believed it to be the voice of the unfettered truth. Point of view, as Kavanagh himself once said, seems to be everything.

From the very beginning Kavanagh enjoyed his growing fame as the mercurial man of contemporary Irish letters. Like the stories he had invented about himself in *The Green Fool*, this pose served to cover up weaknesses in his background and offered a means to get the best of his rivals in a style that appealed to his countryman's instincts. However, this conscious exploitation of pomposity, which began in the late 1930s and lasted to the mid-1950s, had a number of disastrous effects upon his career. It not only alienated various people who could have helped him with jobs and markets for his work during many of his leaner years, but it also hindered his creative development as his concern with image increasingly distracted him from the subjects and themes he had treated so well in his earlier writing. Many of his more sentimental and hollow poems, for example, as well as much of his affected and contradictory criticism can be attributed to his role playing. While he openly admitted the damage this did to his development, Kavanagh laid the blame more on Dublin and his associates of the 1940s than on himself.

By mid-1941 Kavanagh's life had assumed the general pattern it would follow for the next nine years. He wrote poems, articles, reviews, and short stories for a variety of magazines and newspapers in England and Ireland, trying as best he could to support himself with the little money he earned. His luck turned somewhat in September, 1942, when he was given an opportunity to write serially. Up to this time he had been a semi-regular reviewer for the *Irish Times* and had written articles for *The Standard* and the *Irish Independent* but had never had his own column. Now he was hired by *The Irish Press* to write a twice-weekly piece entitled "City Commentary." He chose the pseudonym "Piers Plowman," and in his first article, which appeared in the September 14 number of the newspaper, explained that his intention was to give a countryman's impression of city life for the benefit of his rural friends. For the next eighteen months he attended numerous parades, football games, meetings, and other social events and reported his findings in fairly colorless prose. Occasionally he included light, topical verses to highlight a particularly noteworthy happening.

During the period in which he was contributing to *The Irish Press* he was given the chance to write a second column as the result of articles he had written for *The Standard* about Lough Derg and the pilgrimage to Croagh Patrick. Called "Literary Scene," the series ran for four months, from February 26 to June 11, 1943, and was intended to be a weekly book review. Kavanagh, however, soon began to include comments about the latest happenings in Dublin's literary circles. By April he had nearly abandoned the reviews and was concentrating almost solely on expressing his own views on literature through a number of brief, critical essays. Most of these essays were mild enough, though some, such as "The Road to Nowhere" and "The Anglo-Irish Mind," provoked controversy. Despite his return to straight reviewing by the end of May, he lost his position and was replaced by Benedict Kiely, the novelist.

Three years later, in February, 1946, Kavanagh was back on *The Standard*'s staff. This time he was hired as a film critic. His weekly "Round the Cinemas" column appeared for a little over three years, until July 8, 1949. Generally, his reporting of Dublin's cinema offerings was acerbic and few new films pleased him. As the weeks passed and his initial rage at contrived and artificial plot, dialogue, and situation gave way to boredom, he came to the conclusion that film was an empty medium. From this point onwards he was no longer content to review Dublin's cinema offerings and broadened the scope of his column to include indictments of newspapers and magazines he believed were not presenting a genuine picture of Ireland. He also criticized the cultureless mediocrities, as he called them, who were responsible for producing films, plays, and novels which in his opinion were low, lewd, and illiterate. Although many of his "Round the Cinemas" pieces are filled with plot summaries of what are now old movies, his film reviews are interesting because they reflect his growing concern with literary and social criticism, and serve not only as an indication of the type of crtical investigation that he would carry on later in his monthly *Envoy* "Diary," but also as a mark of his developing vision of himself as a liberating force in Irish art and culture.

Kavanagh continued to write his film reviews until the summer of 1949. In July his column was replaced by an abbreviated film review attributed to an unnamed panel of *Standard* staff. Kavanagh left *The Standard* principally because he had become bored with the material he had to deal with and wished to devote his full energies to the new monthly column at *Envoy*. Entitled "Diary," this column offered Kavanagh a more suitable platform from which to criticize the enemies of literature and culture. After his first "Diary" appeared he wrote that "I am continuing this 'Diary' every month and should succeed in maddening plenty of mediocrities."[11] As might be expected, he maddened more than mediocrities. His constant scourging of writers whom he believed lacked the true nobility of the poet was delivered nonstop in twenty monthly parts, from December, 1949, to July, 1951. Friends and enemies alike, along with complete strangers, were brought before Kavanagh's monthly court and sentenced according to his own peculiar and often contradictory code of literary justice. Austin Clarke, Jack Yeats (painter, writer, and brother of the poet), Frank O'Connor, Sean O'Faolain, James Stephens, John Synge—the list is too long to mention all of the writers cast down from the lofty summit of Parnassus. However, Kavanagh gave praise as well as condemnation in the course of his ordering the house of literature. William Butler Yeats, James Joyce, Ezra Pound, W.H. Auden, and others were treated to commendations.

After *Envoy* ceased publication, Kavanagh, aided by his brother Peter, began writing and publishing his own newspaper, *Kavanagh's Weekly*, in April, 1952. The purpose of this newspaper, as Kavanagh himself stated, "was to introduce the critical-constructive note into Irish thought."[12] The controversial journal appeared for thirteen weeks, from April 12 to July 5, 1952. Throughout this period Kavanagh delivered the kind of bombastic indictments for which he had by now become famous. No aspect of Irish life was spared. His investigation ranged from questioning the need for Irish embasssies around the world to revealing the pathetic state to which gossip had sunk on Grafton Street. Church, government, films, drama, poetry, painting, and other topics relevant and irrelevant to Irish society came under Kavanagh's scrutiny. For all of its bluster and dogmatism, however, *Kavanagh's Weekly* had a certain freshness and wit that made it popular with some and abhorrent to others. The size of its circulation, never large, was kept down more by a lack of proper distribution than by an absence of interest. In the final issue, which was shortened to four pages, Kavanagh featured a long editorial explaining the reasons why the journal was coming to an end. He spoke of a shortage of funds, but emphasized his belief in the lack of a suitable audience, which was, he insisted, the primary reason for stopping publication.

This journal had been Kavanagh's most sustained attempt to illuminate the darkness into which he believed Irish life and literature had sunk; and the fact that it had been an embarrassing failure, proving costly in terms of both money and pride, surely must have stung him deeply. From the mid-1930s, when he began to explore the hollow and futile existence of rural life, through the 1940s, as his investigation broadened to include all of Irish society, to the time of his *Envoy* "Diary," Kavanagh gradually came to believe in himself as a liberating force that could, through exposure and ridicule, open the eyes of his countrymen to the oppressive and stifling provincialism in which they lived. His first pleasure in assuming the pose of the blustery critic led him, by the early 1950s, into carrying on an even more dramatic role as the crusading journalist. To expose the creators of the sentimental and the artificial, the mediocrities, as he termed them, became for Kavanagh not an egotistical game, as many people thought, but a passion that served to direct his creative and critical energies. His mistake, as he later stated in *Self Portrait*, was his gradual acceptance of the belief that this was the poet's goal: to awaken a society deadened to its own best interests. The failure of *Kavanagh's Weekly*, then, unsettled him and foreshadowed the disillusionment he was soon to suffer, yet it did not entirely discourage him from continuing his thrusts at the people he accused of being pseudo-artists.

IV   *The Trial*

While Kavanagh was living in London after the close of *Kavanagh's Weekly* a rather one-sided "Profile" of him was published in the October, 1952, number of *The Leader*, a popular weekly of the day.[13] Kavanagh responded to the piece by hurrying home to Dublin where he filed a libel action against *The Leader*'s publishers. His strong reaction to the "Profile" is interesting for several reasons. While the general tone of the piece is rather derisive, much of what is said about Kavanagh's poetry is complimentary. *The Great Hunger*, for example, is singled out as the finest long poem since Oliver Goldsmith's "The Deserted Village." However, the primary intention of the "Profile" seems to have been, apart from a desire to appraise Kavanagh's literary and journalistic achievements, to render a portrait of the poet in a style that caricatures Kavanagh's own critical mode. As a result, the article frequently borders on ridicule. Yet this manner of summarizing the life and works of a writer is the very method Kavanagh himself practiced and perfected in *Envoy* and *Kavanagh's Weekly*. Instead of being offended, Kavanagh might have considered this piece, which closes by affirming his talent as a poet, as an illustration of the powerful influence his journalism was having on other writers. Had he encountered the "Profile" in different circumstances, had it appeared either before or during the existence of *Kavanagh's Weekly* and not so soon after his journal's demise, when the sting of failure still must have been felt, his reaction might have been different. He might have seen it as a challenge to be countered and rebutted through a clever satire or a skillful essay instead of grounds for libel.[14]

Curiously, nearly everyone who mentions this famous libel action refers to it as "Kavanagh's Trial," as if he were the defendant rather than the plaintiff. Even during the course of the action itself, which opened on February 3, 1954, the case was conducted as if it were Kavanagh rather than *The Leader* who was attempting to prove his innocence. Extensive extracts from the *Irish Times'* account of the trial are included in Kavanagh's *Collected Pruse* and detail the course of the proceedings. Further commentary and grace notes, including the names of the jurors and a list of the contributors to the appeal fund, are given in *Lapped Furrows*. On February 12 a verdict of "not guilty" was returned and Kavanagh was ordered to pay all costs. He did not hear the decision against him, as he was ill and resting in the nearby Four Courts Hotel. When friends brought him the news, he was quite stunned. The following day Kavanagh prepared this statement for the newspapers but on his solicitor's advice did not issue it:

I was not personally shocked by the verdict. I was ashamed of the society in which I live. I was sorry that the vital and gay new Ireland I represented had been repudiated by the old forces of mediocrity, malice and death. I have kept my integrity. It is not I who have lost. This is not the final judgement.[15]

This notice marked one of the most trying moments of Kavanagh's life. Considering his mental and physical condition — he had collapsed in court on the sixth day of the trial after enduring some thirteen hours of severe cross-examination—the shock of losing the libel action affected him deeply. The disillusionment that had begun with the failure of *Kavanagh's Weekly* was now complete. Still, he could not admit to defeat, and chose to see himself as a victim unjustly treated by a society he had hoped to awaken.

The strain of the legal action, his worry about the appeal, and his inability to find steady work all contributed to the general decline of Kavanagh's health. A year earlier he had suffered a severe case of alcoholic poisoning and had been told to refrain from heavy drinking. Now it was discovered that he had cancer of the lung and required immediate surgery. He entered the Rialto Hospital on March 1, 1955, and had the diseased lung removed. He was in very serious condition for several days and many people thought it improbable that he would survive. The *Irish Times* prepared an obituary. Others, friends and former foes, began to prepare for his funeral. Even Kavanagh himself assumed he would not live through the operation and had a will drawn up before he entered the hospital. Despite all of these preparations, as Kavanagh often remarked, he disappointed many people and survived.

V   *Rebirth*

After he left the hospital, Kavanagh spent most of the summer in Dublin, and it was during the months of July and August, 1955, that his famous "rebirth" took place on the banks of the Grand Canal. In the peaceful park-like area along the banks of the canal he had an opportunity to reflect on his life, particularly the dramatic events of the past few years and the goals he had sought to achieve in his writing. The failure of *Kavanagh's Weekly*, the trial, and his recent illness all contributed to mellowing Kavanagh. Though he would write again about the perpetrators of the false and the sentimental, he was never to protest as loudly nor as strongly as he had. In a very real sense the crusading spirit was gone out of him. It was replaced by a second pastoral period, a return to his earlier personal vision but with an added depth that wisdom gives. He no longer fought against himself or the society in which he lived with such forcefulness as in the past. This new mellowness was characterized by acceptance and joy in rediscovering the common and ordinary qualities of life that had made certain aspects of his years in Inniskeen so exciting. The harangues against the philistines were replaced by the story of his personal odyssey which led him to his rebirth on the banks of the Grand Canal.

In June, 1957, Kavanagh began a monthly contribution to *Creation*, a Dublin fashion magazine. This job lasted only a few months, and his articles, on such nonliterary subjects as cooking and bachelorhood, suggest that its brevity was due to the same boredom that turned him away from the similar column he had written for *The Irish Press.* By the spring of 1958 he was again writing serially, this time for the *Irish Farmers' Journal.*

His new weekly column, which appeared regularly until March, 1963, covered a wide range of material. Though he treated certain aspects of farming as well as a number of light literary topics, his favorite subject proved to be his own life. Of the more than two hundred columns that he wrote, over half were about his time on the farm in Monaghan and his many years in Dublin. These pieces were often full of the nostalgia and sentiment that characterize the best and the worst of his poetry.

While he continued his series of weekly anecdotes in the *Irish Farmers' Journal,* he also contributed a column to a new monthly, the *National Observer.* His first article, "On a Column," was published in July, 1959. Kavanagh's observations on social and political issues no longer appeared after January, 1960, perhaps because, unlike earlier years, his views seemed much milder than those of the other writers who contributed. The last serial writing that Kavanagh did was for the *RTV Guide.* By the time he began to write for this weekly entertainment tabloid in 1964, his health and his social conscience were both nearly gone. His television reviews, which appeared off and on from January, 1964, to October, 1966, were mixed with reminiscences about his Inniskeen days and contained little of his former journalistic vigor.

The gradual decline of Kavanagh's health after 1966 had a significant influence on his writing. (The list of physical ailments included thrombosis in the leg, damaged kidneys and liver, heart pains, and ulcers, as well as a debilitating cough brought on by heavy cigarette smoking.) As his physical condition worsened, his desire to write, especially poetry, slackened. The zeal he showed from 1956 to 1961 slowly gave way to despondency. In 1963, for example, he showed little or no interest in selecting the poems for his forthcoming *Collected Poems.*[16] Before his enthusiasm diminished completely, however, he succeeded in arranging for two more collections of his poetry to be published.

From as early as February, 1956, when he sent a collection of his older poems to Macmillan, he seemed intent on regaining the prestige he believed he had lost as the result of his trial. It may seem out of character, considering all that he said on the topic, but throughout his life Kavanagh enjoyed the prestige and publicity he received as a poet and journalist. His frequent disclaimers, such as in his preface to *Collected Poems* and in the various interviews he gave, were nothing more than the exercise of one of his many poses, for he enjoyed notoriety from very early in his career and believed it to be the mark of the successful writer. He was thus keenly affected by the belief that he was ignored by English and American critics. Like most poets, Kavanagh was interested in securing an artistic reputation and achieving critical recognition. His letters, both the early notes to his sister Celia in the 1930s and the long correspondence he carried on with his brother, provide ample proof of this. To regain his prestige, then, as well as to restore his pride, it became highly important for him to publish another book of poetry.

His goal was partially realized in 1958 when his brother published a number of his poems on a hand press in New York. Peter printed several dozen quarto-sized booklets and sent the loose sheets off to Patrick in Dublin. After correcting a number of printing errors, he had the booklets bound and placed for sale in a Dublin bookshop. He titled this small collection *Recent Poems*, despite the fact that several of the poems had been written more than ten years earlier.

Two years later Kavanagh succeeded in publishing a second book. This collection of thirty-four poems was issued in March, 1960, by Longmans under the title, *Come Dance with Kitty Stobling and Other Poems*. Financially, it was the most successful book of poetry Kavanagh had ever published. By November it had been selected as the choice of the Poetry Book Society, had sold over two thousand copies, and was in its third printing. Many of the poems that Kavanagh had given Longmans to fill out the collection dated from the late 1940s and early 1950s. Because of this he never thought very highly of the book himself, though its success was influential in MacGibbon & Kee's interest a year later when they issued him a contract to publish his collected poems.

Had his health allowed it, the 1960s might well have been Kavanagh's most successful creative period. During the years from 1956 to 1960 he wrote some of his finest poetry, and one can only guess at what he might have done had he not suffered from so many physical disabilities. His creative efforts after 1960 were small. His main achievement was his *Self Portrait*, which he wrote for Telefis Eireann in September-October, 1962. While he also made a recording, *Almost Everything*, in 1963 and tried to rework one of his old novels for MacGibbon & Kee, he wrote very little else.[17] By 1964 he fully realized his various illnesses were permanent and wrote to Peter that he was much too ill to produce anything of value, explaining that that kind of work took energy which he no longer had.

His health deteriorated steadily and Kavanagh died on November 30, 1967, at the age of sixty-three. In the months that followed he was honored and praised, and various facets of his life and works were sympathetically recalled in a series of obituaries in Ireland, England, and America. Some of these articles, editorials, essays, and poems celebrated him as the perennial peasant, while others hailed him as the finest Irish poet since Yeats. Ironically, many of the tributes—those that dealt with his authentic "Irishness" and rural proclivity, for example—were the kinds of accolades he raged against most of his life. Perhaps the best obituary of all is his own *Self Portrait*, the last and most important statement he made about his life and his ideas on poetry. Though it offers little information that had not already been published, this small autobiography succeeds in presenting Kavanagh more clearly than any of his other prose works. In fact, it reveals more about him than he may have been aware.

VI   Self Portrait

Self Portrait confirms, first of all, Kavanagh's lifelong penchant for viewing life not as it was but as he wanted it to be, a characteristic of his worst writing from his earliest lyric poems to his final newspaper columns. (Perhaps the most embarrassing example of this lapse in vision is the overly dramatic and contrived ending of *Tarry Flynn*, an otherwise fine novel.) The necessity for role playing is another aspect of Kavanagh's nature that emerges clearly from *Self Portrait*. Here he is momentarily the scourging critic, damning Dublin as that "malignant" city or his fellow writers as "bohemian rascals" or "embittered people." Next he slips into the role of the benevolent essayist and explains that he no longer thinks it necessary to make fierce attacks on foolish poets and storytellers. Between these roles he speaks as the pastoral philosopher, honestly reflecting on what was and what might have been.

Perhaps more important, *Self Portrait* also characterizes Kavanagh in that it illustrates and in some ways explains the confusion that is common to so much of his prose, especially in his criticism and autobiographical pieces. He writes, for example, that his life as a young man on the farm in Monaghan was intolerable, yet he exclaims several paragraphs later that his worst mistake was in leaving that farm, a comment underscored by his claim that he took this action against his will. While Kavanagh was aware of his inconsistencies, he blamed the inadequate audience he found in Dublin as the source of "everything that was loud, journalistic, and untrue" in his writing. However, the real source of his confusion is centered in his opening remark in *Self Portrait* that "the self is only interesting as an illustration." When fact was in opposition to a mood or a vision he wished to express he simply changed the fact to fit the mood or the vision. This accounts for the apparent paradox that results from his advice about the proper subject matter for poems. On the one hand, he instructs his readers in *Self Portrait* that subjects of public importance are not the sort of thing a poet should concern himself with; rather, he should pursue "casual, insignificant things." On the other hand, he ignored his own dictum and devotes much of the book to educating his readers about such subjects of public importance as art and culture. Kavanagh never really adopted a new poetic philosophy, as he suggests in *Self Portrait*, because his ideas about literature in this autobiography are the same ones that give *The Green Fool*, *Tarry Flynn*, and *The Great Hunger* their artistic substance. What he succeeded in producing in this self-portrait was not a clear statement about either his life or his theory of literature, but a demonstration of an intense, intuitive, and highly creative mind that justified its inconsistent view of life and literature by shifting points of view when fact and vision were at odds.

CHAPTER 2

Apprenticeship: 1928 - 1939

AFTER Kavanagh left the farm to practice the literary trade in London and Dublin his countryman's instincts and his original ideas about poetry remained part of him. Poetry was not literature; it was "the breath of young life and the cry of elemental beings."[1] In a very real sense life and literature were so intertwined for him that he could not speak of one without describing it in terms of the other. When he wrote that "an artist, whether poet or farmer, must find glory and exultation in struggling with the crude ungainly crust of earth and spirit,"[2] he not only postulated his philosophy of living and writing in regard to his difficulties in dealing with the demands of his talent during his apprenticeship, but he also demonstrated the close relationship of life to art that is at the heart of his creative expression.

Apart from their own interest, the poems Kavanagh wrote during the period 1928 - 1939 are important because they contain many of the ideas he would pursue throughout his career as a writer. His concern with the meaning and function of poetry, for example, which is common to so much of his creative and critical writing, is one of the themes that dominates his early period. Other themes and subjects, such as rural life and nature, that he would continue to pursue in his later work are also present. Perhaps the most significant of these is his lifelong urge to speak about the nature of the poet and the poet's relationship to the muse and the poetic impulse. This concern is one of the forces that shaped his whole creative and critical career and is thus an important part of the early poetry that demands close examination. In regard to this another of the important aspects of his apprenticeship emerges: the techniques and methods he evolved to express his artistic sensitivity and the life he saw around him. While some of the difficulties Kavanagh encountered, such as his lack of clarity and sense of direction, can be laid to the fact that he was entering into an area of thought and expression that was entirely new to him, a number of his problems

were due to the background from which he began his poetic departure.

It is quite apparent that his early efforts at writing poems were
made difficult by the brevity of his education, the lack of his exposure to literature, and the general low level of intellectual activity
in his native community. These aspects of life in Inniskeen feature
largely in his claim in *Self Portrait* that his childhood experience
was the usual barbaric life of the Irish country poor. According to
Kavanagh, the barbarism of rural poverty lies in the fact that it is a
mental rather than an actual condition. He believed that his own
family, despite their adequate income, was impoverished due to a
lack of enlightenment which, as he says in *Self Portrait*, affected
him deeply.[3] This sense of mental poverty appears to be the main
reason why Kavanagh's formal education was so brief. Since his
parents planned his future for him as a cobbler-farmer there was no
need to send him on in school.[4] More important than this, however,
was the limited reading matter to which he had access during his
early years on the farm. Despite the fact that his father had a
reputation for being more literate than his neighbors, Kavanagh
found very little in the way of literature in his home. Because of
these handicaps he had limited opportunity to train his mind or
develop his talent until he began visiting Dublin in the early 1930s.
As a result, many of his first efforts at serious poetry suffer greatly
from an overromantic conception of what he imagined literature to
be.

I   *Newspaper Poet*

In the period that preceded his apprenticeship Kavanagh wrote
the usual singsong verse that is typical of all schoolboy poets.[5]
When one reads these poems it is difficult to imagine that their
author could write *The Great Hunger*. The opening stanza of "The
Band" provides a typical example:

> That famous society called the Chunk
> I never hear of it today
> For it has into oblivion sunk
> And fled like morning mists away.

The faults here—inverted word order, forced rhyme, and
melodramatic tone—are common to all of Kavanagh's juvenile

poems. "The Shoemaker," written somewhat later, features another
weakness: unadulterated sentimentality—

> Oh see the boots being cobbled while the cobbler
>   sings a song
> About the pleasures of the time when he was young
>   and strong.
> When he could make a pair of boots in less than
>   half a day
> But now his hands are getting stiff and his hair
>   is turning grey.

Still, beneath the forced rhymes, the heavy meters, and the naive
emotion of many of these early creative efforts there are flashes of
comic lyricism and signs of a true poetic impulse which suggest
possibilities for growth. "The Shoemaker" is not a good poem, yet it
prefigures one of Kavanagh's later themes, finding value in performing common and ordinary tasks well.

Though his juvenile poems contain positive elements that
Kavanagh would retain and develop,[6] the poetry he wrote in his
mid-twenties at the beginning of his apprenticeship shows little real
growth in the handling of themes and ideas. Kavanagh himself was
embarrassed by this work and once remarked:

I am fully aware of how embarrassing self-revelation can be. In my head
there is the woefullest anthology of bad poetry, and for many years I have
been terrified lest this mangy cat of my youth's bad taste might escape from
the bag.[7]

The "bad taste" he refers to here are those poems he published
between September, 1928, and June, 1929, in the *Irish Weekly
Independent*'s "Poet's Corner."[8] Yet these early publications contain certain characteristics that dominate his poetic apprenticeship.
His concept of the proper pose a poet should assume, for example, is
clearly suggested in "A Pure White Scroll":

> The past is dead and we stand beside
>   The door of a golden Dawning.
>
> Faith's lifted her lamp on a mystic height,
>   Bright angels are watching over us.
> Nought matters now but the words we write
>   On the pure-white scroll before us.

Kavanagh probably adopted this melodramatic pose from the poetry he read in school. He recalls in *The Green Fool* that his literary education did not include living poets and that his school reader contained nothing by those who were bringing about a renaissance in Irish letters. Instead, his experience with serious poetry was limited to a few selections from the works of Walter Scott, Alexander Pope, Alfred Tennyson, James Clarence Mangan, and Joseph Campbell. His favorite poet was Thomas Moore, whose influence is quite apparent in the highly emotional language of his early poetry. His rather juvenile concept of poetry was also undoubtedly reinforced by the verse that he read in his father's old almanacs and religious magazines. However he came to form his ideas about poets and poetry, his description of himself in *The Green Fool* as a pious poet during these early years is an understatement.

Perhaps the most interesting of Kavanagh's early creative efforts are his love poems. Such verses as "The Pessimist," "Freedom," and "Till Love Came" are all too sentimental and contrived to be successful love poems, yet like so much of this early material they suggest directions of development. "Freedom," in addition to foreshadowing the love poetry he would write in the early 1930s, describes the joy that knowledge gained from awareness can give a troubled mind and includes a motif, the escape through reverie to a world of fulfilled dreams, that appears in a number of other apprenticeship lyrics. Other love poems are didactic and feature a device Kavanagh employed when he felt the urge to moralize. To emphasize a point, he frequently addressed himself to a child, who in his earliest poems usually lacked poetic sensitivity but who later became one with his own poetic consciousness. In "To a Child I Know," for example, he acknowledges his debt to a child for reminding him of the beauties of life, whereas the child he speaks to in the earlier "To All Children" requires enlightenment from the poet to find true goodness and happiness in life.

His Inniskeen surroundings, as well as love, the poetic process, and the powers of the muse, provided material for his newspaper poetry. In selecting subjects for these local-color poems, Kavanagh chose aspects of his surroundings that he thought had the proper romantic spirit. He wrote two poems about the local tinkers because their life on the road appealed to his imagination and corresponded to his idea of suitable subject matter. His approach in both poems is not very original. He admits in *The Green Fool* that "The Tramp

Woman" was inspired by Padraic Colum's "An Old Woman." The unfortunate creature in Colum's poem is near despair:

> Och! but I'm weary of mist and dark,
> And roads where there's never a house nor bush,
> And tired I am of bog and road,
> And the crying wind and the lonesome hush!

Kavanagh's tinker seems to be the same poor soul a little further down the road:

> A road that for her had no ending,
> Her shoulders neath a wearisome load
> Earthwards were bending.

In "The Rich Tramp" Kavanagh strikes a lighter note and celebrates the casualness of tinker life. The poem also indicates that Kavanagh had begun to focus on local events, situations, and activities as departure points for his investigation of the relationship between life and art.

Of all the poems that he wrote during the first part of his poetic apprenticeship perhaps the best is "Thralldom" because it clearly presents the most crucial difficulties he encountered in developing his talent. In the first stanza:

> Oh! must I ever struggle here,
>   Murmuring faintly to the throngs
> Who cannot hear, or will not hear,
>   My sorrow laden songs?

he sets out the problem of communicating the knowledge that he is gaining with the aid of the poetic muse through his sensitivity. Like Robert Frost, Kavanagh has discovered the essential difference between the poet and the nonpoet, the distinction between those who understand the meaning of revelation and those who do not, and he is troubled by the isolation such a distinction can impose on him. At the same time he ponders the possibilities for satisfying his strong impulse to carry the search for truth even further:

> . . . shall I ever wander forth
>   Across the wide, unknown expanses
> To learn the secrets of the earth
>   And linger where romance is?

> To muse where mighty spirits rose
>   In learning's great and radiant morning,
> And calm the soul that overflows
>   With philosophical yearning?

The tension between his fear of isolation and his desire to pursue truth is heightened by his realization of the restrictions, both physical and psychological, that his environment is placing on him. To perceive, interpret, and teach are the goals he is striving for, yet he is frustrated in his attempts to achieve them because his rural situation, with all of its inherent disadvantages, holds him fast, as he points out in the poem's final stanza:

> But, Fate! Then hast declared that I
>   Must grovel here, and wear thy chains.
> There is no sunshine in my sky,
>   No flower on my plains.

In the midst of what must have seemed a most difficult situation, Kavanagh discovered the existence of a literary world far larger than the one he had been moving in and one which immediately offered him hope. The source of this opportunity, of course, was his chance discovery of AE's the *Irish Statesman* in a Dundalk newspaper shop. In a short while he advanced from subscriber to contributor and in the process became acquainted with AE himself. Soon he also was buying and reading such other literary magazines as *The Dublin Magazine* and *Poetry.* What he read in these periodicals confirmed the doubts about his own poetry, particularly its lack of substance, its artificial language, and its melodramatic tone.

II   *Important Influences*

Kavanagh's acquaintanceship with AE between 1929 and 1931 furthered his literary career in several important ways. It was AE who introduced him to the literary world of Dublin and London by publishing "The Intangible" (October 1929) and "Dreamer" and "Ploughman" (February 1930) in the *Irish Statesman.* When Kavanagh visited Dublin in 1930 AE invited him to his home and, after tutoring him on literature, sent him back to Inniskeen with a large supply of books. In addition to such Irish writers as Thomas Moore and James Stephens, AE's gift included novels by Victor

Hugo and Feodor Dostoevsky, collections of poems by Walt Whitman, Robert Browning, Petrarch, and Ralph Waldo Emerson, and an anthology edited by Mahata Sargu, as well as a copy of Kahil Gibran's *The Prophet*. From his letters of this period it seems that Kavanagh read through his small library with great interest. He was impressed with Petrarch's love sonnets, Moore's *Confessions of a Young Man*, and Dostoevsky's *The Idiot*, and praised what he saw as the emotional warmth of Hugo's writing. James Stephens's poetry paled, he thought, on the second reading. While he did not believe in the philosophy he found in *The Prophet*, he imitated Gibran's ethereal manner in several of his own poems. Rather curiously he did not see a great deal of merit in either Emerson's prose or Whitman's poetry. He may have been sickened, as he claims in *The Green Fool*, by Emerson's "transcendental bunkum," but the influence of Emerson's doctrine of the oversoul is quite apparent in a number of Kavanagh's poems about nature. In a similar manner, while he did not praise Whitman's literary achievement, the influence of Whitman's celebration of the common man is clearly evident in certain poems about ploughmen and tinkers.

AE's own poetry, however, was even more influential as a source of new themes and approaches than the books he gave Kavanagh. In particular, AE's thoughts about transcendentalism, mythology, and various Eastern philosophies impressed Kavanagh, and he tried to affect a mystic pose in some of his own poetry. "The Intangible," which AE himself liked, is an interesting example. In the second stanza:

> Not black or blue,
> Grey or red or tan
> The skies I travel under.
> A strange unquiet wonder,
> Indian
> Vision and Thunder.

we see Kavanagh attempting to create a mysterious aura about himself. The poem also shows the infuence of AE's style. Because Kavanagh had already employed dreams and visions in his newspaper poetry, he readily adopted AE's manner of beginning a poem with a description of nature that leads, through the operation of vision, to a mystical revelation in the final stanza. "The Intangible" follows this technique closely, with Kavanagh evoking a world of shadows and half-lights where dreams and visions become the mode of enlightenment. He practiced this technique in a large number of his poems and, as he altered and refined it, it became a characteristic of some of his best work.

Kavanagh's interest in modern poetry was also heightened by reading literary periodicals. Of these, *Poetry* was one of the most important in his development because it published a large variety of poetic styles. Spreaking about this in *The Green Fool* Kavanagh recalled that

> I read the work of Ezra Pound and Hopkins with delight. Walter Lowenfels, a poet who made queer verses about machinery, gave my imagination a lift forward. But it was in the American poets I was chiefly interested. Horace Holley, H.D., Gertrude Stein, and all the Cubists and Imagists, excited my clay-heavy mind. Gertrude Stein's work was like whiskey to me, her strange rhythms broke up the cliché formation of my thought.[9]

The names of Carl Sandburg, e.e. cummings, and Edna St. Vincent Millay should be added to this list. Sandburg may have been one of the sources of Kavanagh's early poems about cities, such as "Phoenix." Millay's poetry, which was so popular at this time, appears to have served as the model for some of Kavanagh's own love poems. And some interesting imitations of e.e. cummings's experiments with language appear in several of Kavanagh's early unpublished poems, particularly in these lines from "The Hour":

> Beware! If the gong clangs
> On your passivity
> Narrow despair is grinning
> Mandarin.

But the strongest influence from *Poetry* on Kavanagh's writing was Imagism.

His education in Imagism, he mentions in a letter to his brother Peter, came from the review section of the magazine as well as from the poetry it published.[10] Though he never wrote a poem as thoroughly Imagistic as William Carlos Williams's "The Red Wheelbarrow," he did adopt much of the Imagist creed as originally put forward by Ezra Pound: to use the language of common speech and employ the exact rather than the decorative word; to make full use of free verse; to present an "image," i.e., to render particulars exactly and not deal in vague generalizations; and to write poetry that is hard and clear, free of indefinite statements.[11] Kavanagh believed that Imagism was valuable because "It paints pictures telling us of the beauty perceived through the senses but does not comment on this beauty. It praises by showing."[12] This technique of presenting rather than explaining became one of the strongest forces in his poetry because it offered him the surest method of dealing objectively with materials that otherwise could sink into sentimentality. "June Evening" is typical of his early experiments:

> A tired horse out on grass,
> Goats on a hill,
> A tinker driving an ass
> By the corn mill.

In these lines he succeeds in presenting in simple language a series of clear images that work together to paint an evocative country scene. "Tinker's Wife," written in free verse, is even more successful in following the principles of Imagism and, unlike his earlier tinker pieces, limns a sympathetic portrait of a woman picking over a trash heap that does not suffer from either superfluous decoration or contrived emotion:

> Her face had streaks of care
> Like wires across it.
>
> She searched on the dunghill debris,
> Tripping gingerly
> Over tin canisters
> And sharp-broken
> Dinner plates.

The common words that Kavanagh uses to paint this portrait are more concrete than the abstract phrases we find in either "Thralldom" or "The Intangible." There is no unnecessary description, and the rhythm of his presentation fits the language and the subject. The last three lines of the first stanza, which depict the quality of the woman's movements over the dunghill, create an exact image that neither requires nor receives further comment from the poet and thus prepare the way for the perception of beauty that Kavanagh conveys so objectively in the last stanza. This method of praising by showing, which he does so well here, demonstrates the ultimate value of Imagism to his early development.

Other important influences came from the group of writers Kavanagh met on his visits to Dublin during the early and mid-1930s. One of these new acquaintances was Seamus O'Sullivan, then editor of *The Dublin Magazine*, who offered him an opportunity to publish his poetry in an important journal. O'Sullivan's own poetry interested Kavanagh and he wrote several poems similar to O'Sullivan's in mood and style. Of these, "Gay Cities" particularly suggests the influence of O'Sullivan's belief in the poetic aspects of city life. However, Kavanagh did not feel at home in Dublin and his city poems reflect his countryman's sense of uneasiness in urban surroundings.

More influential than O'Sullivan was Frank O'Connor, the master of the short story, who was at this time translating Gaelic poetry. By 1934 he had become one of Kavanagh's closest Dublin friends, and like AE proved to be a major force in shaping Kavanagh's literary development. O'Connor frequently read Kavanagh's poems and offered valuable criticism. It was his advice, for example, that led Kavanagh to broaden his treatment of rural subjects by altering the vantage point from which he presented his tinkers and ploughmen. Kavanagh acknowledged his debt to O'Connor in "To a Child" when he wrote: "this high dunce/ Had laughter in his heart and eyes . . ./ Ere a Corkman taught him to be wise." The poem concludes with a declaration to continue the investigation of life and art in light of a newly acquired knowledge:

> O child of laughter, I will go
> The meadow ways with you, and there
> We'll find much brighter stars than know
> Cold Aldebaran or the Bear.

The appearance of this poem indicates a significant advancement in Kavanagh's method of treating materials. From 1935 onwards he concentrated on perfecting the honest, controlled vision that manifests itself in the later work of his apprenticeship and in *The Great Hunger*. The growth of a more objective critical insight into life that O'Connor's influence hastened in Kavanagh's thinking was thus typical of the effect that his discovery of modern literature had upon him. It provided the necessary stimulus to make him rethink many of his ideas about poetry and offered him new techniques to clarify his expression of already familiar material. His declaration to "go/ The meadow ways" and search out "brighter stars" was a public announcement of his desire to examine in greater detail and in a less emotional manner the nature of rural life so as to afford a keener perception than his past efforts had produced.

III   Ploughman and Other Poems

Kavanagh's apprenticeship culminated in the publication of *Ploughman and Other Poems* in 1936. Comprised of thirty-one poems written between 1930 and 1935, the book offers a revealing view of Kavanagh's strengths and weaknesses during the middle and later years of his apprenticeship. It not only details his various subjects and themes, but it also documents the various adjustments he made to correct problems in technique and craft. The book marks an important stage in Kavanagh's literary development. He had moved from his first ventures into newspaper verse through a lonely period of self-education to acceptance by the writers who composed Dublin's literati of the day. In addition, the book offered him a place from which he could continue his growth into poetry.

Of all the subjects Kavanagh treats in *Ploughman* few appealed to him as strongly as the nature of poetry. Its complexity interested him throughout his life, but it was in his apprenticeship that he pursued the subject with the greatest zest. He devoted considerable portions of *The Green Fool*, for example, to expounding his views on such matters as the poet's nature, the powers of the muse, and the creative process itself. The idea of poetic sensitivity was particularly interesting to him, and some knowledge of what he had to say about it in his autobiography is helpful in understanding his earlier poems on such matters as the poet's nature and his relationship to society.

Kavanagh's discussion of poetic sensitivity in *The Green Fool* tends to focus more on how it affected his relationships with his family and neighbors than on its nature. While he defined its essential quality very simply:

In those days [i.e., the late twenties] I had a vision. I saw upon the little hills and in the eyes of small flowers beauty too delicately rare for carnal words.[13]

he went to great lengths to explain how it complicated his life. Typical is a sketch about being discovered in the midst of his poetic musings one day by a passing farmer who chastised him for wasting time:

He made me feel that I was just a lazy fool, that all my dreams of beauty and love were only codology. By the heels he pulled me down from the stars and made me a worm-cutter.[14]

Further experiences like this prompted him to vow that he would never again speak about the properties of poetry nor let anyone catch him at its practice. Of course, he did not keep his vow, but incidents such as this were largely responsible for the rather naive image he formed of himself as a poet: a superior though lonely man, possessing secret knowledge only other enlightened or gifted souls could share and appreciate. Though his poetic pose had some basis in truth, he was the only member of his community with a gift for poetry, his over-romantic imagination so enlarged and embroidered the matter that it soon evolved into a role he could play whenever he felt inspired. As his talent matured and his interest in literature developed, he maintained his pose with poems about the distinction between the poet and the nonpoets. "Pygmalion" is perhaps the best of this type. He also wrote a considerable number of poems expressing the suffering his poetic isolation caused him. "April Dusk" is typical:

> It is tragic to be a poet now
> And not a lover
> Paradised under the mutest bough.
>
>   . . .
>
> An unmusical ploughboy whistles down the lane
> Not worried at all about the fate of Europe
> While I sit here feeling the subtle pain
> That every silenced poet has endured.

The issue at stake—what the whistling ploughboy does not comprehend—is the power of loneliness. Though this idea is treated with an embarrassing degree of contrivance and sentimentality here, this aspect of Kavanagh's pose was valid, and he accurately sensed that when the imagination is continuously frustrated it soon becomes numbed and its power neutralized. He feared this and, while he played up loneliness and humiliation as part of his lot, he fought hard not to succumb to these twin dangers of rural isolation. He celebrates his trumph over them in "Inniskeen Road: July Evening":

> I have what every poet hates in spite
> Of all the solemn talk of contemplation.

> A road, a mile of kingdom, I am king
> Of banks and stones and every blooming thing.

In other poems, "I May Read," "Aescetic," and "Dreamer," to name only a few, he reaffirms his belief in the power of his talent and the glory he believes it will bring him.

In the middle of his apprentice period this interest in the poet's nature occasioned a desire to analyze the creative process. Because Kavanagh believed that the faculty to perceive was closely linked to the ability to express, with both functions dependent upon inspiration as the motive force, he concluded that the poet, despite his special sensitivity, could write his poems, express his visions of beauty, only if he was properly inspired. Such a theory of poetry is ultimately based upon a belief in the muse as an almost spiritual power, an idea which no doubt appealed to Kavanagh's strong romanticism because it suggests that the poet, through his relationship with the muse, is capable of being raised to a supernatural level of consciousness. This mystical aspect of his poetic system is clearly reflected in Kavanagh's choice of metaphor when writing about the muse's power and influence over the poet. In the earliest stage of their relationship, for example, the muse performs certain functions not unlike those of the Holy Ghost:

The gods of poetry are generous . . . they let [the poet] take one peep into every tabernacle; they give him transcendent power at the start and ever after he must make his own magic. While he is learning the craft of verse and getting ready his tools they present him with wonderful lines which he thinks are his own. [15]

After this initial infusion of creative grace the poet who wishes to continue making his own "magic" must stay on good terms with the muse. To do this, he is required to court the muse's favor, even pray to it if it becomes necessary. Kavanagh conducted himself accordingly and, as the poem "Worship" indicates, was willing to perform the required adoration when he felt in need of sacramental refreshment: "To your high altar I once came" and said "Open your tabernacles. . ./O cut for me life's bread, for me pour wine!" In "Poet" he presents himself as literary cleric who, in going about the business of recording inspired revelations, is separated from the pleasures of the world by the restrictions his poetic vocation imposes on him. His choice of "monk/ In a grey cell" connotes the nature of the poet's isolation and underscores his dedication.

In regard to this personal aspect of the creative function

Kavanagh believed that the mystical, enlightening quality of poetic vision was as elusive as it was vital and should be a secret shared only with other sensitive and perceptive souls. While he no doubt formed this belief as a defensive mechanism, partially to protect himself from the psychological pressures brought to bear on him in Inniskeen as the result of his first publications, and partially to justify his occasional failures to voice his inner feelings, it was no less real to him. He considered imprudence the primary sin by which the poet could suffer a temporary lapse of perception or expression. In *The Green Fool* he recounts an occasion when a lack of prudence brought about a loss of poetic vision:

I caught glimpses—through the impurities of glass—of that transfigured hill the dreams of poets and children climb . . . I would not dream of mentioning anything rare and innocent in the market-place. I understood that there are things not to be mentioned under the penalty of loss. [But] I told of that beatific wonder to clods and disillusioned lovers. I asked them if they didn't see something beyond the hills of Glassdrummond. They laughed and said I was mad. And I saw no more. I had sinned. [16]

In such circumstances Kavanagh could give full rein to his romantic imagination and envision himself cast down from the lofty role of priestly poet and sentenced to suffer the punishment of being outside the muse's grace.

In other poems he chooses a considerably different metaphor to carry on his discussion of poetry. In such poems as "Ploughman," "Four Birds," and "March" he portrays the poet as a pagan rather than as a priest. This particular metaphor may seem strange, considering that Kavanagh believed "poetry to be a piece of earth in which the Holy Ghost is manifest," [17] yet it gave his concept of the poet greater dimension because it provided him with another vantage point from which to view the poet's relationship to his community and to nature. In "To a Blackbird" he presents the poet acknowledging his paganism:

> O pagan poet you
> And I are one
> In this—we lose our god
> At set of sun.

The relationship between man and bird springs from a shared understanding of nature's special beauties, which are symbolized by the sun. They also share the act of praising; the bird by his song and the poet by his poem. And, like pagans, they both worship natural phenomena, the source of the spiritual force which enlightens them. Finally, the bonds that link them are strengthened by the isolation their belief imposes on them.

> We dream while Earth's sad children
> Go slowly by
> Pleading for our conversion
> With the Most High.

The gentle irony of sad, earthbound children praying for their conversion underscores the fact that the enlightenment they share, which lifts them above these petitioners and enables them to enjoy a happier existence, is unique to them.

The poet as pagan is treated in a number of other poems. In "Blind Dog" Kavanagh traces his quest for the knowledge he appears to possess in "To a Blackbird." Like a maddened astrologer he searches the heavens with "a passionate pagan's desire" for "the truths that are." In "Ethical" he warns the nonbelievers that

> you who have not prayed
> The blackbird's evening prayer
> Will kneel all night dismayed
> Upon a frozen stair.

"To Knowledge" contains a Christian's lament for his pagan days:

> I knew the speech
> Of mountains, I could pray
> With stone and water. O foul leech
> That sucks truth's blood away!

And "A Prayer for Faith" sets out the pagan's creed:

> O give me faith
> That I may be
> Alive when April's
> Ecstasy
> Dances in every
> White-thorn tree.

In the midst of his pagan excitement Kavanagh wrote that "real

poetry is more religious than prayer,"[18] suggesting that only
through the pagan's concrete experience of perception and expression could man understand the truths of life.

The attraction that Kavanagh found in this pagan motif as a
mode for conducting his analysis of the creative process was due to
several developments in his philosophy of life and poetry during the
early 1930s. The idea of the pagan as artist no doubt appealed to
him because he felt himself isolated from his family and neighbors
by his belief in literature just as the pagan is set apart from Christian society by his faith in natural phenomena. Another reason why
this motif seemed apt is brought out in "Kestrel," from the poem
"Four Birds." Here we are told that the kestrel is "a true artist"
because "His art is not divorced/ From life/ And death." In other
words, the pagan ideal supported Kavanagh's belief that the basic
truths his poetic sensitivity allowed him to perceive in the life taking place around him were more real to him than the abstractions
that characterize Christianity. His concept, then, of the natural
order of things, like the pagan's religion, is based on what he can
see and feel, "the touch kingdom," as he explains in "The Sen-
sualist," rather than on what he is told to see and feel.

Perhaps the strongest appeal of paganism, however, was due to a
period of doubt in regard to Catholicism that Kavanagh passed
through when he was in his late twenties. His letters of the period
1932 to 1934 reveal that he no longer considered himself a practicing Catholic. He wrote in May, 1934, for example: "I think quite
a lot of praying (orthodox) has no more spiritual value than a
Dipper's bath."[19] In another letter he comments that "lots of
deliberately religious writing has no real spiritual beauty at all.
That's why many avowed Catholic writers leave one cold."[20] *The
Green Fool* corroborates this falling out with the Church, though in
a rather light-hearted manner, with references to his identification
with the less zealous attendants at Sunday Mass and his dislike of
the evening rosary.

The vision of the poet as pagan might also be explained as having
been the logical outgrowth of one of Kavanagh's other major concerns during his apprenticeship: the theme of nature as explicator.
This theme, common to much of his writing, underlies many of his
first serious poems, such as "The Intangible," where he hears
"ghostly poplars whisper to/ A silent countryside," and a number of
his later poems, such as "Pygmalion," where he sees "Stone ditches

. . . like serpents coiled." The clearest expression of nature's explicatory power appears in one of the untitled lyrics he sent to the English poet John Gawsworth in 1938:

> I know that I have heard spoken
> A different wisdom as
> The tree was shaken
> Above the parlour grass.
>
>   . . . I a fool taught
> By earth to know.[21]

Kavanagh believed that nature was the primary teacher of life's truths and mysteries and thus one of the basic sources of poetry. Attempting to clarify this, he wrote in *The Green Fool*, "Turning over the soil, our fingers were turning the pages in the Book of Life. We could dream as we gathered the potatoes, we could enter in the secret places where all unwritten poems lie."[22]

He seemed particularly attracted to nature's lessons about theological and philosophical matters. In "Primrose" he describes how a flower "lighted me to heaven":

> Upon a bank I sat, a child made seer
> Of one small primrose flowering in my mind.
> Better than wealth it is, said I, to find
> One small page of Truth's manuscript made clear.

In "April" he explains how he saw "in the green meadows/ The maiden of Spring . . . with Child/ By the Holy Ghost." Nature also teaches him other lessons, serving as a type of seasonal catechism for the sensitive man, posing questions and revealing answers about many things. In "After May" he is shown "A light that might be mystic or fraud" playing "on far hills beyond all common sight." "A Wind" reveals something more concrete:

> I see brightly
> In the wind vacancies
> Saint Thomas Aquinas
> And
> Poetry blossoms
> Excitedly
> As the first flower of truth.

But flowers and trees are the principal instructors who explicate the
"Book of Life," and it is primarily from observing them that
Kavanagh learns nature's hidden truths. They invite him to look at
the natural wonders which stimulate the imagination and open the
way to knowledge. A spring flower, as Kavanagh explains in "To a
Coltsfoot Blossom," is "not/ A flower at all/ . . . but a gap/ In
Winter's wall" through which he sees "the faith/ Of a saint of
God." In a similar manner, a leafless tree covered with ice is more
than a barren trunk, it is a window to another world:

> Yesterday I saw the Earth beautiful
> Through the frosted glass of November's tree.
> I peered into an April country
> Where love was day-dream free.[23]

The point to which all of nature's teachings are directed is contained in "Shancoduff." Here we are told the story of a poet-farmer
who surveys his rather stark holdings and appraises their worth in
spiritual rather than in financial terms. The local cattle-drovers see
no real value in his black hills; and from all outward appearances
this seems an accurate judgment. Yet the poet realizes that for all
their apparent unattractiveness they possess a special beauty. They
may not get enough sunlight to produce good crops but they have
served as his Matterhorn and have taught him the wonders with
which nature endows even the bleakest of her creations. The theme
of this poem, then, that life can be made more meaningful through
an appreciation of the subtle beauties present in one's surroundings,
is the principal lesson that nature teaches the sensitive observer.

This knowledge is supplemented by the enlightenment gained
from performing common, ordinary tasks well. Most of Kavanagh's
apprenticeship poems about rural activities deal with the spiritual
value of such work as ploughing and planting. "Ploughman," for
example, features the joy that is realized in preparing a field for
sowing. Through this activity the ploughman becomes an artist who
shares with nature the glory of creation:

> I turn the lea-green down
> Gaily now,
> And paint the meadow brown
> With my plough.

His work allows him to see "a star-lovely art/ In a dark sod." The act of ploughing, rather than being a dull task, becomes an enriching experience that makes him one with nature and offers him an insight through his art into the meaning of life. This theme is also treated in "To the Man after the Harrow," though the approach is somewhat different. In this poem the poet assumes a didactic pose and, instead of merely celebrating the joy of the task at hand, explains just how to benefit from performing it well. He instructs the man behind the harrow to "leave the check-reins slack" because "destiny will not fulfill/ Unless you let the harrow play." In other words, unless the man behind the harrow lets himself be taken by the task and believes in what he is doing his seeds will not be covered nor will he be enlightened. The point of the poem, as in "Ploughman," is that the sensitive man who is in communion with his work can lift his labor to the level of art and thereby find the truths of life made clear. Such themes of enlightenment from nature and from common, ordinary manual tasks, along with the investigations of poetic sensitivity, the nature of the poet, and the creative process, were the main concerns with which Kavanagh dealt in *Ploughman and Other Poems.*

The book also indicates how well Kavanagh had succeeded in solving what he believed to be one of his most serious creative flaws. The chief source of his trouble, he believed, was that his "poetic idealism was suffering from religious mania."[24] This mania, born in part from his romanticizing the nature of the poet and the creative process, manifested itself principally through vague, abstract statements which rang hollow and hindered the clear expression of his ideas. To correct this weakness in his writing Kavanagh began to practice what he called "objective reality," changing the poet's function from seer to simple observer. Such a shift in function, he hoped, would enable him to avoid the subjective language that was diluting the substance of his poetry. His goal was to follow more closely the techniques he saw practiced in the best poems he had read.

To maintain "objective reality" Kavanagh made a number of specific adjustments to his method of treating materials. This involved retaining and developing some of the techniques he had already employed successfully as well as experimenting with new ways of presenting themes and ideas. The most important technique he retained was dramatic description, or as he phrased it, praising by showing. To increase its effectiveness he began to use figures of speech, particularly metaphor, simile, and personification,

in more effective ways. Typical of his experiments is "The Chase,"
a short lyric about the pursuit of wisdom:

> I went quickly
> As gulls over fallow,
> As goats among crags,
> As winds through a hollow.
>
> Yet never I
> Caught up with slow-footed
> Wisdom who took
> The lanes deepest rutted.

Although this is not one of his better poems, it indicates how he
attempted to employ simile and personification specifically to give
his sense of failure real proportion. By emphasizing the physical act
of pursuit rather than abstract properties of wisdom he communicates the quality of his experience clearly and concretely. This
is a significant improvement over the vagueness of such poems as
"The Intangible," "Soft Ease," or "Ascetic." However, Kavanagh's
greatest success in using figures of speech and concrete language to
advance his technique of dramatic description came in his treatment of rural life. In "Burial Service," which commemorates the
death of his first horse, "the kicking mare" of *The Green Fool*, he
successfully employs language to present a ceremony that in earlier
poems might well have occasioned a flood of sentimental emotion.
The first stanza begins with the factual statement that the twenty-
seven-year-old mare is dead, then continues with a description of
the burial itself, which is objective yet suggests the quality of feeling Kavanagh had for the horse:

> We buried her where
> The brown turf-mould,
> Free from stones,
> Presses little
> On her sapless bones.

The language is sharp and clear and evokes in the reader's imagination an image of the dead, stiff horse lying under the brown sod and
an idea of the care with which it was buried. In the second stanza
Kavanagh concludes his presentation by focusing on other specific
details:

> We marked the spot
> With a smashed spade shaft.
> It was not Evening. We laughed
> At a cruel tale
> A peasant told
> Of a woman crushed and pale
> And not old.

Melodrama and sentimentality are avoided through the use of these details, which create a realistic scene and reflect the emotions and attitudes of country people in their performance of a necessary ritual. Kavanagh does not comment on what has taken place as he would have in his earlier poems; instead, he leaves the reader to reflect on the implication of the peasant's tale at the careful burial of a dead horse.

In the course of his experiments to develop techniques that would enable him to give his poetry a sense of objective reality Kavanagh evolved a new approach to the subject of self-analysis, one which combined his previous investigation of the nature of his talent with his belief in nature's explicatory powers. This new approach was based on the relationship he felt existed between himself and his surroundings. He theorized that by examining various aspects of the world in which he lived he would find revealed to him certain truths that would give him a more thorough understanding of himself as a man equipped with poetic sensitivity. To carry out this examination he approached his subjects in such a way as to mirror the specific qualities that characterized them and that revealed some aspect of his own personality. He explains this new approach in "Mirrors":

> Everything I look upon
> I make
> A mirror of
> Wherein to see my soul in all its seasons.

Kavanagh used this method of mirroring his surroundings to reflect aspects of his own image quite successfully in a number of the poems he wrote after 1935. In "Monaghan Hills," for example, he sees his faults reflected in the low hills that border his farm: "O Monaghan hills when is writ your story/ A carbon copy will unfold my being." Despite their number they are all too small to grow crops of any value. Recognizing this he reflects that

> The country of my mind
> Has a hundred little heads
> On none of which foot-room for genius.

Somewhat naturalistically he blames the hills for his being "a half-faithed ploughman/ . . . a beggar of song/ And coward in thunder." Musing on how life might have been had he been "born among the Mournes,/ Even in Forkhill," he concludes that

> I might have had echo-corners in my soul
> Repeating the dawn laughter.
>
> I might have climbed to know the glory
> Of toppling from the roof of seeing.

"Memory of My Father" features a totally different environment in which he sees reflections of himself. In Dublin and London he holds his mirror to capture images of himself as his father's son:

> That man I saw in Gardiner Street
> Stumble on the kerb way one,
> He stared at me half-eyed,
> I might have been his son.
>
> And I remember the musician
> Faltering over his fiddle
> In Bayswater, London,
> He too set me the riddle.

IV *Double Vision: the Legacy of* Ploughman and Other Poems

The development and use of these two techniques, dramatic description and mirroring, indicate the directions that Kavanagh's poetry took during the last stage of his apprenticeship. Knowing the dangers of easy emotion and abstract language, he no longer tried to treat all of his themes and ideas in the same style nor with the same techniques. Instead, he began to focus his poetic vision in two distinctly different directions in order to accommodate his continuing investigations of the self and the nature of rural life. To pursue self-analysis he adopted a subjective view that focused through introspection on various aspects of his personality. This inner view was balanced by an outer view that was objective and focused through exposition on rural life. The operation of this double vision distinguishes the two types of poetry that he wrote after 1935. In such poems as "Pursuit of the Ideal," "In the Same Mood," and "Ploughman,"[25] we see the inner vision focusing on his personal struggles with his talent and with his fate as a ploughman-poet. "The Irony of It," a typical example of the inner vision in operation, catalogues his problems and comments on his inability to solve them. He states at the beginning of the poem that "The complexes of many slaves are in my verses." Elaborating, he acknowledges that

> I have not the fine audacity of men
> Who have mastered the pen
> Or the purse.
>   . . .
> I see talent coldly
> Damning me to stooped attrition.

The poem continues with a lament over his failure to sort out personal difficulties and ends with a protest against his poetic burden:

> It was not right
> That my mind should have echoed life's overtones.
> That I should have seen a flower
> Petalled in mighty power.

Because of its objectivity, the outer vision, though not as intense, is frequently sharper and often more balanced than the inner vision. "Peasant Poet," for example, in addition to serving as Kavanagh's proclamation of the outer vision, presents a clearer picture of human struggle than does "The Irony of It." Announcing that he is "the representative of/ Clay-faced sucklers of spade-handles," Kavanagh proclaims "their history is a grain of wheat." He views peasant Ireland as "a race that will persist/ When all the scintillating tribes of Reason/ Are folded in a literary mist." In other poems, "The Hired Boy," "Christmas Eve Remembered," and "My People," in particular, he focuses on the peasants' strengths, joys, and sufferings and communicates these observations in language that demonstrates the power of his vision.

While this double vision characterizes the poetry that Kavanagh wrote during the last stage of his apprenticeship, it also foreshadows his future involvement with social and cultural criticism. As he developed these two points of view, and as his talent matured, he expanded his investigation of rural life into a broader study of Irish culture, focusing at various times on the artistic, political, and social aspects of modern Ireland. The themes and techniques that he concentrated on between 1935 and 1940 were to become the basic motifs and modes of this investigation which reached its peak in the late 1940s and early 1950s. Like many of the writers whose works formed the basis of his literary education, he believed that the way to self-knowledge, the chief motive for nearly all of his excursions into literary and cultural criticism, lay in understanding the individual's relationship to the society in which he lives. The importance of this belief to Kavanagh's developing ideas about poetry is apparent in *The Green Fool*.

V   The Green Fool

That he chose autobiography as the form for his first venture into prose demonstrates his intention to realize the meaning of his own identity. This book, which marks his transition from apprentice-poet to professional writer, is charged with great energy and illustrates the excitement and enthusiasm he had for life and literature during the time he lived in Inniskeen. But more important than his enthusiasm is the use he made of his materials. Throughout the book imagination overpowers fact. Places, events, and people are interesting to him because they provide the background against which his own personality can be revealed. Kavanagh makes his neighbors symbols of his countryside; they absorb their surroundings so that in his relations with them they serve to illuminate facets of the relationship he senses between himself and his environment.[26] His imagination transforms them into mirror-like figures, reflecting aspects of his own existence. In a similar manner, his imagination embroiders certain events as well as creates others to give his life a greater sense of drama than it had. His justification of this, that "there is not much drama in real life"[27] is an admission of the strong romanticism that prevents *The Green Fool*, as it hinders his early poetry and frustrates much of his later writing, from advancing his investigation of the self.

This romanticism is manifested in the various poses that Kavanagh assumed in the course of his apprenticeship, culminating in his role as the green fool, the wise ploughman-poet who laughs at his spiritual isolation. Because he chose to see life not as it was but as he would like it to be, all of his attempts at honest self-appraisal seemed doomed. Instead of coming to know himself he merely succeeded in creating a series of roles and poses that suited his changing impressions of the world in which he lived and reflected the appropriate intensity of his romanticism. The problem that Kavanagh failed to solve until late in his life was that there was a significant difference between what he believed and what he actually saw, felt, and thought. As a result, he continued to shift from self-pity to self-esteem in his quest for identity and in time succeeded in confusing even himself as to what was real and what was imagined. *The Green Fool* sets out this problem of the romantic versus the real and prefigures the tangled thinking from which so much of his later poetry and criticism suffers.

Some of Kavanagh's difficulties with these matters may well have been due to the influence of Frank O'Connor and Sean O'Faolain. O'Faolain, for example, believed during the mid-1930s that Irish writers, because of the turmoil of contemporary Irish life, should not be judged too harshly if their work seemed confused and disorganized. He announced in the *Irish Times* that

The whole social picture is upside down, and we do not know where we are or what is real or unreal, what clashes are arising in it, what values are really being followed in the lives of the people. Every Irish writer of to-day over thirty is a spiritual *deraciné*.

Because of this breakdown in the social order, O'Faolain considered realism doomed, and suggested that the Irish writer turn to romance and fantasy and concentrate on reorientating into himself.

. . . for there alone in his own dark cave of self can he hope to find certainty of reality. And being, perforce, divided by his interest in life and his retirement into self, he must be forever seeking . . . a solution to the antinomies within him, a possession of his Ego, a unity of being.[28]

These ideas no doubt fitted smoothly into the theory of poetry that Kavanagh had been constructing for himself since his first poems appeared in the *Irish Weekly Independent* in 1928. Surely he must have felt that O'Faolain's thesis both supported his own ideas about the split in his poetic vision and indicated his close kinship to the new group of writers emerging out of postwar Ireland.

CHAPTER 3

The Great Hunger: 1940 - 1942

THE publication of *The Great Hunger* in 1942 marks one of the high points of Kavanagh's literary career. Internationally acclaimed as one of the twentieth-century's better long poems, this dark portrait of Irish country life secured Kavanagh's reputation and demonstrated his growing concern with cultural criticism as a means for understanding the nature of the human soul. Though he spoke out against certain aspects of the poem late in his life, there is little doubt that *The Great Hunger* is Kavanagh's most successful and sustained literary effort. The poem chronicles the life of Patrick Maguire, a lonely sixty-five-year-old bachelor farmer, a peasant Everyman whose existence symbolizes the subtle but debilitating paralysis that can render an entire society impotent.

I *Sowing the Seeds*

The Great Hunger was not Kavanagh's first attempt to depict the rigor, frustration, and ultimate despair that characterized certain aspects of peasant life in his day. Nor was it his first effort at detailing the difficulties and dangers that a restricted experience posed for the sensitive man. Earlier, even before he began writing "Stony Grey Soil" in 1938 (his first novel about the complexities of country life), he treated these aspects of rural environment in his apprenticeship poems and in *The Green Fool*. As early as 1929 in the rather juvenile "Thralldom" his sense of being oppressed by his environment is apparent. The proposition that he advanced late in his life, "that courage, gaiety, wisdom and so forth derive from the right kind of soil,"[1] suggesting that there is something in the land itself that affects the people who live on it, is manifest in his earliest poetry. It was on this belief that he based his judgment in *The Green Fool* that "there is no humanitarianism among folk who live close to life."[2] Their primitiveness, both spiritual and intellectual, is a reflection of the world they inhabit. The land dominates their lives, influencing their behavior and their actions. If the soil is bad, as it is in that area of County Monaghan where Kavanagh lived, then it frequently renders those who live on it powerless to improve their condition. This idea, one of the major themes of *The Great Hunger*, is the subject of "My People," an early experiment in dramatic dialogue which appeared in *The Dublin Magazine* in 1937. The first speaker, a Stranger, opens the dialogue with a question:

> What kind your people are
> I would wish to know[?]

then goes on to reflect that they appear to him to be

> Great-shouldered men like rolling stock,
> Great in despair,
> Simple in prayer,
> And their hard hands tear
> The soil on the rock
> Where the plough cannot go?

The Stranger's impression, which Kavanagh suggests is typical of the outsider's misunderstanding of the peasant, is corrected by the second speaker, a Poet, who declares simply that " 'Tis not so," and remarks that the land has enslaved his people, broken their spirits, and forced them into an existence that offers neither hope nor satisfaction. Though "My People" is not one of Kavanagh's better poems, it is interesting because it brings together the desire to portray the reality of country life with the need to teach the outside world about the specific qualities that make the peasant a tragic figure. These concerns, developed separately in such early poems as "Burial Service," "Furrow," "Peasant Poet," and "Plough Horses," merge in *The Great Hunger*.

Like the best of his apprentice poetry, *The Great Hunger* was fashioned from Kavanagh's own experiences as a small farmer as well as from observations of his neighbors. The combination of memory and imagination, which contributes so significantly to the lifelike proportions of the poem's characters, indicates that Kavanagh, unlike some Irish poets who chose country scenes and situations merely as a mode of expression, was capable of writing directly about rural Ireland with accuracy and understanding. His use of landscape and setting was not a contrivance to affect an Irish pastoral quality in his poetry; rather, it was a sign of the direction his quest for identity had taken and an affirmation of his belief that the surest course to self-understanding and unity of being lay through an exposition of his environment. Patrick Maguire is a composite of those beliefs, hopes, and fears that Kavanagh recollects in *The Green Fool* when he explains the world of his youth.

Maguire's tie to the land springs directly from Kavanagh's own sense of agricultural bondage, a phenomenon that appears in several early poems, such as "Plough," where a plough becomes a symbol for the seductive power the land has over the farmer:

> Plough, take your thin arms from about my middle,
>   . . .
> Release me, release me, my desires would run
> In the shallower furrows of passion.

The implication here, of course, is that the harvest the poet desires is sexual, not agricultural. The land's power is too strong, however, to be neutralized by a mere cry of protest:

> O clinging, possessive mistress, O plough
> Though I break your hold your charms
>   possess me still.

This sexual metaphor is effectively repeated again in *The Great Hunger* where it underscores the tragic irony of a man who brings his fields, rather than his body and his soul, to fruition.

The awareness of this bondage increases the desire to escape from the monotonous cycle of farm life. By the late 1930s, with the prospect of escape that his talent offered him, Kavanagh's own sense of rural bondage began to shift from a personal to a larger, more social concern. It was principally this broadening of vision that enabled him to transcend his own experiences and portray the objective realities of peasant life.

In choosing the narrative rather than the personal voice for *The Great Hunger*, Kavanagh seems to have been influenced by some of the poetry he had read during his apprenticeship. A case in point is Joseph Campbell's *Irishry* (1913), a collection of poems depicting various rural characters. There are some interesting similarities between Campbell's portraits and certain descriptive passages in Kavanagh's poem. The description of Maguire as a man who worked "a fourteen-hour day . . . for years" sitting before the fire with "his legs over the impotent cinders" is similar to Campbell's sketch of an old farmer who "For fifty years . . . trenched his fields" and "now sits with folded hands/Over the flag of amber fire." *The Great Hunger*, however, is not only a more penetrating examination of the peasant's existence, but it is also a harsher appraisal of his world than Campbell's *Irishry*. This is due to the fact that Kavanagh was writing about a subject of which he had keen knowledge and certain personal prejudices. This, coupled with the strength of his talent, enabled him to write a poem that is as powerful as it is original.

II *The Bitter Harvest*

When *The Great Hunger* opens Maguire is already an old man and the reader is invited to look on as Kavanagh presents the physical scene and the mental attitudes that have shaped Maguire's life and turned his youthful dream into an old man's nightmare. The images conveyed in the first lines immediately create an atmosphere of gloom that will be sustained throughout the poem:

> . . . the potato-gatherers like mechanized scare crows
>   move
> Along the side-fall of the hill—Maguire and his men.
> We will wait and watch the tragedy to the last
>   curtain,
> Till the last soul passively like a bag of
>   wet clay
> Rolls down the side of the hill, diverted by the
>   angles
> Where the plough missed or a spade stands,
>   straitening the way.

Maguire knows he has lost the struggle for life. He may rationalize his situation, comforting himself with the thought that he is the wisest man in the townland, a man who has come "free from every net spread/In the gaps of experience," but it is only pretense. Despite occasional gestures of independence, he suffers the flaw of passive acceptance. His life has been reduced to a dull pattern of farm chores and familial obligations by a series of submissions to his mother, to the land, and to the Church.

The poem dramatizes Maguire's flaw by developing a fine tension between his outer appearance and his inner thoughts. He is as deceptive as the society he comes to represent. In directing his men harvesting the autumn potatoes, he acts with authority and knowledge:

> ˙Move forward the basket and balance it steady
> In this hollow. Pull down the shafts of that
> cart, Joe,
> And straddle the horse . . .˙

But in his mind he is less sure of himself and wonders as he surveys the withered potato drills before him "if his mother was right/When she praised the man who made a field his bride." For most of his life he has had the appearance of the successful farmer. In his youth he demonstrated a proper suspicion of young women and refused to be drawn into sin by their cries of passion. He could sit on a wooden gate and smoke a cigarette knowing that he had a pound to spend and that "His cattle were fat/ And his horses all that/ Midsummer grass could make them." As he grew older

> He looked like a man who could give advice
> To foolish young fellows . . .
> And there was depth in his jaw and his voice
> was the voice of a great cattle-dealer.

He was accepted and admired by the parish priest and his fellow farmers and, appropriately, he affected a judicial stance, suggesting respectability and righteousness. Behind this pose, however, was fear and uncertainty.

In time the stifled passion of his youth became an insatiable hunger that he attempted to satisfy by masturbation and dreams of seduction, activities which reinforced his loneliness and passivity. Caring for his farm became the chief means of soothing his inner frustrations. Still, his fourteen-hour day was more a retreat from life than a show of ambition. While the drug of labor deadened his misery it proved to be a temporary balm. Its effectiveness was lost as he realized that his work in the fields compounded his difficulties and locked him more securely into a cycle of existence from which he could not escape:

> He would have changed the circle if he could,
> The circle that was the grass track where he ran,
> Twenty times a day he ran round the field

> And still there was no winning-post where the
>   runner is cheered home.
> Desperately he broke the tune,
> But however he tried always the same melody crept
>   up from the background,
> The dragging step of the ploughman going home
>   through the guttery
> Headlands under an April-watery moon.

There were moments, however, when he perceived beauty and wonder in his surroundings:

> The yellow buttercups and the bluebells among
>   the whin bushes
> On rocks in the middle of ploughing
> Was a bright spoke in the wheel
> Of the peasant's mill.
> The gold finches on the railway paling were
>   worth looking at—
> A man might imagine then
> Himself in Brazil and these birds the birds
>   of paradise
> And the Amazon and the romance traced on the
>   school map lived again.

But such visions were "Too beautifully perfect to use" and, though they served as pleasant distractions from monotonous toil, they were bittersweet reminders of his unobtainable dreams, heightening his misery and undermining his spirit. While he might comfort himself by stroking the flanks of his cattle in lieu of a wife to fondle, or sit up half the night playing cards with neighbors, when he sat alone before his fire eating a chunk of wheaten bread and drinking a cup of cocoa he was confronted with the harsh reality that for him

> There [was] no to-morrow;
> No future but only time stretched for the mowing
>   of the hay
> Or putting an axle in the turf-barrow.

Despite his disillusionment and his sufferings, Maguire does not become despondent or hardened. His sister, Mary Ann, may acknowledge defeat and scream in despair that she is "locked in a stable with pigs and cows forever," but he accepts his fate.

Miserable and without hope, he retains patience and endures. He lights the fire in the morning, gives the cows their hay, and continues to tend his fields. In turn he becomes more Christian as he accepts the futility of his life. His relationship with his neighbors, for example, grows more tender and sympathetic:

> He helped a poor woman whose cow
> Had died on her;
> He dragged home a drunken man on a winter's night;
> And one rare moment he heard the young people
>   playing on the railway stile
> And he wished them happiness and whatever they
>   most desired from life.

In her bitterness, his sister calls him soft and chastises him for giving the local children pennies and caramels. Perhaps his actions are due in part to sentimentality, in part to the wisdom one can gain from experiencing defeat. Indeed, the long years he spent in the fields opened his mind to many things in addition to his personal troubles. He seems to have learned a set of values that might have saved him had he had such knowledge in his youth, though he discovered too late that the five senses are a better guide to life's truths than the absolutes his youthful dreams envisioned. Had he snatched a kiss here, a laugh there, instead of desiring all or nothing, he might have been more successful in satisfying his hunger for life. But he failed to act and chose to wait, letting himself believe that time would answer his prayers for marriage and money.

Out of the knowledge that time does not bless, Maguire comes to accept his fate and finds solace in the thought that death can be no worse than life. Yet his acceptance is also his final submission to those forces that have restricted his manhood. Accordingly, he lives out his days so "that his fields may stay fertile when his own body/Is spread in the bottom of a ditch under two coulters crossed in Christ's Name." His tragedy is complete:

> He stands in the doorway of his house
> A ragged sculpture of the wind,
> October creaks the rotted mattress,
> The bedposts fall. No hopes. No lust.

While Magure is the poem's central figure, he is only one of the characters in this sad drama. The presence of his mother, sister, and neighbors serves as a means of comparison by which his own failure may be more fully understood and adds depth and dimension to the environment in which the action takes place. His mother is a strong woman who fails to communicate her strength to her children. Ninety-one when she dies, she senses the weakness her overprotectiveness has produced in her children and spends her last hours confessing this fear to the local priest. Maguire's sister is even more pathetic, living with one leg in hell, the other in heaven, and her soul suspended in "the purgatory of middle-aged virginity." Her passion for life is stronger than his, and venting her frustration after her mother's death, she cries out: "Who bent the coin of my destiny/ That it stuck in the slot?" The neighbors, while less developed, complete the gloomy world where "crows gabble over worms and frogs" and "gulls like old newspapers are blown clear of the hedges." They share the same amusements and dreams that Maguire enjoys. In the evenings they collect either at the crossroads where "Heavy heads [nod] out words as wise/As the rumination of cows after milking" or in the local pub where they are "all savants by the time of pub-close." Like Maguire, they are victims of an existence that offers few opportunities for growth and fulfillment.

III   *A Dark Landscape*

In a sense, the world of *The Great Hunger* is as much a state of mind as it is a physical environment for the peasant. With an interesting play upon a familiar biblical expression Kavanagh begins his description of this world by explaining that here "Clay is the word and clay is the flesh." The peasant's intellectual energy, like his physical stamina, is drained from him by the clayey soil to which he gives his life. Yet the land is not the only force with which he must contend. The psychological conditions under which he functions also contribute to his failure to achieve a full life. Indeed, the grip the irregular fields have on him is strengthened by the strictures of his spiritual beliefs and the social mores of his community. This fact is stressed throughout the poem. A horse may lift its head "To lip late passion in the crawling clover" but when the peasant sees "girls sitting on the grass banks of lanes" he must shut his eyes "for that sight is sin." True manhood is denied him:

> The cows and horses breed,
> And the potato-seed

> Gives a bud and a root and rots
> In the good mother's way with her sons;
> The fledged bird is thrown
> From the nest—on its own.
> But the peasant in his little acres is tied
> To a mother's womb by the wind-toughened navel-cord
> Like a goat tethered to the stump of a tree[.]

Because of this he lives like "half a vegetable/Who can react to sun and rain" and "remember what man is/But there is nothing he can do." In time he resembles "A sick horse nosing around the meadow for a clean place to die," though his illness is more mental than physical. This is why he does not fear death. Figuratively, he is half-dead already, and, as Kavanagh explains, he will feel no differently after he dies than when he was alive and walked through his native village. He suffers from a form of psychological paralysis that renders him impotent and turns his life into tragedy.

In Maguire's case this paralysis is brought on by the pressures of social custom, religious belief, and agricultural bondage. Social custom dictates that he submit to his mother's will and forego marriage, remaining a bachelor until the farm becomes his outright. Yet, by keeping a tight grip on him, his mother fails in her maternal duty and restricts his passage into manhood. Instead of forcing him to act on his own so that he may develop a sense of personal responsibility, she reinforces his passive acceptance and contributes to his mental emasculation. The very length of her life has a negative effect on him, for the longer she lives the deeper her paralyzing influence cuts into him:

> It cut him up the middle till he became more
>   woman than man,
> And it cut through to his mind before the end.

It is his mother who tells him that the wise man makes a field his bride. While she lives, she sees to it that he has no need for a wife by mending his clothes, cooking his meals, and tending to all other wifely matters save that of satisfying his sexual hunger. "Wife and mother in one," as Kavanagh terms her, she manages his life in the same way as she directs the farm:

> She held the strings of her children's Punch and
>   Judy, and when a mouth opened

> It was her truth that the dolls would have spoken
> If they hadn't been made out of wood and tin.

However, his mother means well. For all her power, she, too, suffers from the paralyzing forces of the peasant's environment. She senses the danger of her strong grip on her son and trusts "in Nature that never deceives" to enlighten him. But he is held closely and taught too well to understand the meaning behind her words, taking them as literal truth until it is too late.

The Church, like his mother, should be a source of guidance and enlightenment, serving as a positive force in his attempt to achieve a full life. Instead, it too paralyzes him by corroborating his mother's warnings about temptation, sin, and the damnation that awaits the man foolish enough to follow his natural impulses. In place of life's pleasures he is awarded the honor of holding "the collection box in the chapel door/During all the Sundays in May." He is not strong enough to act for himself. When he is presented opportunities for physical pleasure, he yields neither to the push of nature nor to the morality of common sense. The Church's teachings and his mother's preachings thus combine to ensure his failure to satisfy the hungers that his body and spirit suffer.

As great as these two forces are, the power the land has over him is greater because agricultural bondage is a stronger tie than either blood or faith. The roots that feed his heart come from the land, not from his mother or his religion. He is, in a sense, the flesh made clay. In fact, by the end of *The Great Hunger* Kavanagh makes it clear that it is this close relationship between peasant and land that ultimately damns Maguire. The relationship is almost mystical in its intensity. It is not in the communion service, for example, that Maguire sees divine mystery manifest but in a tree, where God the Father is the trunk, the Holy Spirit is the rising sap, and Christ the bright leaves that will come at Easter. At Mass his mind dwells on his fields: "Wonder should I cross-plough that turnip ground." His mental flaw, his passive submission and the resulting denial of his own natural instincts, is born of the centuries of life on the land. He is not the master of his fields, he is a servant ministering to them, compounding his servitude with each new crop he plants. In this way his life is sacrificed so that his fields may remain fertile and yield a harvest while his own manhood withers away like the weeds he pulls from the potato drills. His achievements are measured by the seeds he has sown and the crops he has harvested rather than by the children he has fathered or by the fortune he has made.

IV   *Craft and Technique*

The successful presentation of this penetrating study of peasant life proves that by 1942 Kavanagh could execute as well as conceive a work of major proportions. The poem achieves its depth and sustains its forcefulness because of a skillful handling of the technical and dramatic details that unify its presentation. While Maguire's presence dominates the poem, serving as an obvious unifying element, other devices aid in binding the poem's fourteen sections together. One such device is the subtle comparing and contrasting of the slow decay of Maguire's life and the shabbiness of his world with the regenerative cycle of nature and the beauty of its various seasons. Very early in the poem this unifying tension is created when October's symphony on a slack wire paling is contrasted with Maguire's lonely surveillance of his lifeless fields. This tension is sustained by references to seasonal changes, which both note the passing of time and document Maguire's growing disillusionment. Direct description supplements this use of nature to portray the peasant's landscape. Finally, by employing synecdoche throughout the poem, Kavanagh is able to select precisely the exact image that will evoke the scene.

The poem is also unified by the simple repetition of certain actions, images, and metaphors. Maguire's hapless act of flinging a stone into the air in section I is repeated in section V where a boy, bored with the dullness of an evening at the local crossroads, throws a piece of gravel on to the railway. Sometimes it is a single image that is repeated to emphasize a particular quality of peasant life. The sense of agricultural bondage that haunts Maguire, for example, is described in terms of the endless cycle of planting, sowing, and harvesting. In section IV the reader is told:

> He would have changed the circle if he could,
> The circle that was the grass track where he ran.

The image appears again in section IX:

> He gave himself another year,
> Something was bound to happen before then—
> The circle would break down
> And he would curve the new one to his own will.

and in section XIII:

> Like a goat tethered to the stump of a tree—
> He circles around and around wondering why it
>   should be.

Descriptions of various animals and birds, used to detail aspects of Maguire's shabby world, provide a reoccurring motif to heighten the impact of certain scenes. In the opening lines of section I the images of "A dog lying on a torn jacket under a heeled-up cart" and "A horse nosing along the posied headlands trailing/A rusty plough" contribute to the pathetic picture of Maguire and his men moving like scarecrows over the fields. Further on in the poem details like a dead sparrow lying on a tattered waistcoat or an old horse searching out a clean place to die reflect the spiritless mood that has settled on the aging Maguire. Of all the descriptive devices that are repeated in the poem the most common is the metaphor that mirrors the peasant's sexual frustrations. This metaphor is introduced in section I when Kavanagh explains that

> Lost in the passion that never needs a wife—
> The pricks that pricked were the pointed pins
>   of harrows.

The metaphor occurs again in section III: "The twisting sod rolls over on her back—/ The virgin screams before the irresistible sock." Both planting:

> They put down
> The seeds blindly with sensuous groping fingers,

and harvesting:

> Turn over the weedy clods and tease out the
>   tangled skeins,
>   . . . his mud-gloved fingers probe in this
> insensitive hair. . . .

become means by which the peasant can direct his energy into his small acres and attempt to find release from his sexual agony. Thus, the repetition of this metaphor underlines the irony of a culture that produces fertile fields but impotent men.

The dramatic quality of *The Great Hunger* is kept at a high level by the fine use of flashback, direct and indirect characterization, and dialogue. Of these, the flashback is perhaps the most skillfully employed. It is through a series of flashbacks that the reader is shown Maguire's failure and how it is brought about. The device is particularly effective in a long narrative poem because it enables the poet to be highly selective in his choice of materials: in this case those facets of Maguire's life that detail his condition and turn him into an Everyman of the peasant world. As the reader is shown glimpses of him struggling with temptation, enjoying himself in the pub, or going about his farm duties, the vision is colored by the knowledge that he is a doomed man. Because of this, the poem reads like history and the reader's attention is directed toward detail. It is, of course, the details that Kavanagh wishes to emphasize; for it is only by comprehending them that the reader will come to understand the forces that shape the peasant's world.

The flashback is coordinated with an equally successful use of dramatic description to link the various passages together. Sometimes this description is delivered in a simple, straightforward manner to depict a particular scene:

> A man stood beside a potato-pit
> And clapped his arms
> And pranced on the crisp roots
> And shouted to warm himself.
> Then he buck-leaped about the potatoes
> And scooped them into a basket.
> He looked like a bucking suck-calf
> Whose spine was being tickled.

At other times it is combined with bits of interior monologue to convey moments of personal insight on the part of the poem's characters:

> Mary Anne came away from the deathbed and
>   boiled the calves their gruel.
> O what was I doing when the procession passed?
> Where was I looking?
> Young women and men
> And I might have joined them.
>
>   . . .
>
> I remember a night we walked
> Through the moon of Donaghmoyne,
> Four of us seeking adventure,
> It was midsummer forty years ago.
> Now I know
> The moment that gave the turn to my life.
> O Christ! I am locked in a stable with
>   pigs and cows forever.

Description is also mixed with either dialogue or fragments of conversation to create verisimilitude:

> [The pub] was their university. Maguire was an
>   undergraduate
> Who dreamed from his lowly position of rising
> To a professorship like Larry McKenna or Duffy
> Or the pig-gelder Nallon whose knowledge was amazing.
> 'A treble, full multiple odds . . . That's flat porter . . .
> My turnips are destroyed with blackguardly crows . . .
> Another one . . . No, you're wrong about that thing I was
>   telling you . . .
> Did you part with your filly, Jack? I heard that
>   you sold her . . .'

The various combinations of dramatic description not only allowed Kavanagh to vary the rhythm of his narrative, but they also provided for direct characterization. Other narrative sections of *The Great Hunger* feature reflective passages, providing still another way in which to relate detail but also achieve the illusion of viewing that detail from a different vantage point. In this way, then, by shifting rhythms, altering vantage points, and utilizing dialogue and interior monologue, Kavanagh managed to alter the pace of the narrative while continuing to focus the reader's attention on individual details until a complete picture is created that communicates the full tragedy of Maguire's life. The final effect is not unlike the technique of the modern film, with background subordinated to the central figure but treated in such a way, through close-ups, longshots, and skillful editing, as to achieve an organic unity of all the parts and so heighten the overall effect of the piece.

V   *Light Out of Darkness*

In presenting his study of the peasant's existence, Kavanagh preaches what he believed was an important lesson about the reality of rural life. In section XIII of the poem he points out that the tourist or the occasional traveler envisions the peasant as an idyllic creature:

> The world looks on
> And talks of the peasant:
> The peasant has no worries;
> In his little lyrical fields

> He ploughs and sows;
> He eats fresh food,
> He loves fresh women,
> He is his own master.
>   . . .
>
> His heart is pure,
> His mind is clear,
> He can talk to God as Moses and Isaiah talked—
>   . . .
> The peasant is the unspoiled child of Prophecy,
> The peasant is all virtues— . . . .

Of course, this vision of rural life is a distortion due to a lack of knowledge and a false sense of perspective. The world looks on from the outside and thus sees only a dream of pastoral bliss, not "the blood of life-as-it-is lived." To correct this distortion Kavanagh forces his reader to see significant differences between outward appearance and inner reality.

The reader's reward is not the temporary refreshment a traveler feels who stops for a moment to look at the countryside, but a more enduring, spiritual enlightenment born of a sympathy for and an understanding of the peasant's ordeal. To clarify this truth Kavanagh explains:

> Let us be kind, let us be kind and sympathetic:
> Maybe life is not for joking or finding happiness
>   in—
> This tiny light in Oriental Darkness
> Looking out chance windows of poetry or prayer.
>
> And the grief and defeat of men like these
>   peasants
> Is God's way—maybe—and we must not want too
>   much
> To see.
> The twisted thread is stronger than the
>   windswept fleece.
> And in the end who shall rest in truth's high peace?
> Or whose is the world now, even now?

The answer, the poem implies, is the strong—those people who endure. This is both the knowledge and the comfort that can be gained from realizing the peasant's position; for Maguire, despite his flaws and failures, accepts his fate. In this spirit Kavanagh invites us to

> . . . kneel where the blind ploughman kneels
> And learn to live without despairing
> In a mud-walled space—
> Illiterate, unknown and unknowing.

By including this philosophical lesson in *The Great Hunger* Kavanagh was indirectly protesting the manner in which certain English and Irish writers had treated rural life. The implication here is that only those poems, plays, stories, and novels that penetrate into the suffering heart and soul of rural Ireland render an honest portrait of the subject. In criticizing the tourist or the occasional traveler who, having viewed the ploughman in his fields, mistakes his life for pastoral bliss, Kavanagh suggests that those writers who celebrate the unreality of country life are guilty of sentimentality and misrepresentation because they either lack proper vision or fail to look closely enough. In either case they have failed in their treatment and, as he would later phrase it, they have created a lie. This concern for authenticity was already part of Kavanagh's literary credo when he wrote *The Great Hunger*. And, while he would later become more vehement in his criticism of writers who did not depict the peasant accurately, he had already begun to chastise those who contented themselves with what he thought were false portraits of Irish life.

Perhaps a more important motive behind *The Great Hunger* was Kavanagh's desire to clarify for himself his relationship to the culture that shaped his artistic consciousness. This urge to examine the self as a product of a specific physical and psychological landscape manifests itself again and again throughout his literary career. From his earliest newspaper verse to such last poems as "Living in the Country" and "The Poet's Ready Reckoner" he sets about the task of interpreting the world of his experience in order to understand more fully the meaning of his spirituality and poetic sensitivity.

By 1940 he had begun to develop a sense of perspective in regard to his life in Inniskeen that is different from the view presented in either *The Green Fool* or in his apprenticeship poetry. This shift in view, occasioned by his move from the farm to Dublin, was intellectual as well as artistic. During his early years in the city he came to see his adolescence and young manhood less subjectively than he had viewed them earlier. While he became more sentimental about certain aspects of his past, he became more critical of the land. These changes in the treatment of his rural experience are apparent in the five poems he published shortly before he wrote *The Great*

Hunger in late 1941. Generally, all five poems are sentimental reminiscences that support his claim in *Self Portrait* that at this time he was purposefully affecting a ploughman pose to exploit the image his first two books had created for him. "A Christmas Childhood," for example, is a romantic recollection of an Inniskeen Christmas in 1910. He describes the winter beauty of the family farm and recalls that

> My father played the melodeon,
> My mother milked the cows,
> And I had a prayer like a white rose pinned
> On the Virgin Mary's blouse.

Despite its fine lyric quality the poem has little depth. "Kednaminsha," "Art McCooey," and "Spraying the Potatoes" also suffer from a similar lack of substance. As occasional pieces and celebrations of romantic rural scenes they have their merits, for they all feature vivid imagery and evocative language as well as demonstrate a firm control of emotion which saves them from sinking into saccharine sentimentality. In addition, "Art McCooey" utilizes colloquial expression to lend authenticity to the depiction of Kavanagh's horse-and-cart days.

Of the five poems only "Stony Grey Soil" goes beyond his ploughman pose to reveal a genuine quest for the self and to offer an appraisal of the land's influence on him. He views his life as a cobbler-farmer less favorably in this poem than he does in the other four. This darker view foreshadows the somber mood that characterizes *The Great Hunger*. In fact, it would not be wrong to say that "Stony Grey Soil" serves as a preface to *The Great Hunger* by introducing that antagonism toward the land, born of bitterness and frustration, that dominates *The Great Hunger's* final stanza. But the most important aspect both poems share is Kavanagh's concern with how his life on the land has affected his artistic development. He poses this question in "Stony Grey Soil" when he asks:

> O can I still stroke the monster's back
> Or write with unpoisoned pen
> His name in these lonely verses [?]

The answer is yes and no. When he wrote occasionally, as he did in "A Christmas Childhood" or in "Spraying the Potatoes," his pen was free of poison. However, when he probed his background more seriously, as in *The Great Hunger*, traces of prejudice appeared in respect to the material he selected and on which he commented.

In *The Great Hunger* he continued this practice of focusing on the less pleasant aspects of rural life. There is no real hope for the peasant, only the empty consolation that no one who lives in the country escapes the land's restricting influence. While Kavanagh is sympathetic to the peasant's position, he concludes that the land, the Church, and the social order which both give rise to are destructive elements too powerful to be combated successfully. This conclusion is at the heart of his unfinished novel, "Stony Grey Soil," and its revision, *Tarry Flynn*. The only manner of escape from the peasant's fate of intellectual paralysis and spiritual emasculation is to leave the countryside. This is the solution put forward in *Tarry Flynn*. By leaving the land physically one could then hope to escape from it intellectually as well. Of course, this is what Kavanagh did in 1939 when he made his permanent break with Inniskeen and moved himself to Dublin. By writing *The Great Hunger* from the distance of Dublin he succeeded in sorting out for himself many of the restraints under which he had labored during his apprenticeship and in so doing freed himself from their influence. He could now focus the critical faculty of his poetic vision more fully on other facets of his experience.

CHAPTER 4

Quest and Commitment: 1943 - 1954

I The Shaping of a Career: Influences

L IKE the poetry Kavanagh wrote during his apprenticeship, the work he produced during the period following the
publication of *The Great Hunger,* from the early 1940s to the mid-
1950s, is marked by certain outside influences and inner forces that
combined to shape the substance of his literary output and direct
the course of his creative growth. Of the outside influences, the
most important were his literary friends and rivals and his efforts to
earn a living by writing. Daily contact with such writers and journalists as Frank O'Connor, Sean O'Faolain, Peadar O'Donnell,
Robert Farren, Austin Clarke, and R. M. Smyllie, to name only a
few, served as a source of stimulation and provided frequent opportunities to exchange ideas about life and literature.

From discussions with O'Connor, for example, Kavanagh was encouraged to continue the pursuit of cultural criticism. He embraced
his mentor's concern about the dangers of intellectual strangulation
at the hands of the government and the Church. *The Great Hunger*
itself, though not the first, was perhaps the best of his ventures into
a sustained appraisal of Irish life. Like O'Connor, many of
Kavanagh's other friends, such as Sean O'Faolain and Peadar
O'Donnell, encouraged him to examine the harsh realities and
restrictions of Irish society. In this spirit of cultural investigation
and exposé he began to comment with increasing vigor on many
aspects of Irish life and letters, giving particular attention to the
pseudo-literature he believed writers like Austin Clarke and Robert
Farren were creating. Though this criticism was controlled and subdued at first, it gradually became highly vitriolic and, on occasion,
somewhat irrational. Before the tide of his critical enthusiasm
ebbed, his targets and exposés included even those friends who
had helped him through his transition from ploughman-poet
to professional writer.

Kavanagh's commitment to literary and cultural criticism and its ultimate effect on the development of his poetry was furthered by the journalism he wrote during these middle years. For economic reasons, from 1940 to 1952, he devoted much of his time and energy to periodical prose, producing numerous reviews and articles in addition to four serial columns. Despite the fact that this writing frequently was done at the expense of his creative work, it did contribute to the growth of both his critical and creative powers because the materials he reviewed exposed him to the variety of ways in which a writer could treat human experience. Of course, not all of the material he dealt with was of a high literary quality. Indeed, the books he reviewed for the *Irish Times*, for example, ranged from scholarly studies of writers like George Bernard Shaw, Gerard Manley Hopkins, and W. H. Auden to sentimental romances about Victorian England and esoteric tracts about witchcraft. While no special skill was required to appraise these latter works, such books as Denis Devlin's *Lough Derg and Other Poems* and Graham Greene's *Thirteen Stories* demanded a specific knowledge of literary craft and genre. As a result, in the early years of his foray into literary criticism he was forced to educate himself in both the theory and the technique of literature. By late 1944, when he was reviewing as many as three and four books a week, he considered himself one of Ireland's best critics. In the course of establishing his criteria he began to reexamine his approach to the various themes and subjects he treated in his own writing and so initiated a process of creative readjustment directly related to the development of a firm critical stance.

The impact that his journalism had on his creative impulse was a major factor in bringing about a change in his poetry. No longer did he consider poetry principally as a means for expressing his personal struggles with his environment, his past, and his artistic sensitivity. Now he turned to it as a vehicle for his emerging critical voice. The lyrical, personal voice that had evolved during the years of his apprenticeship was now supplemented by a didactic, public voice. While both voices are present in *The Great Hunger* and, to a lesser degree, in some of his early poems, it is in this middle period that his public voice is at its most intense. In a sense, during the 1940s and early 1950s the double vision that characterizes the last poems of his apprenticeship separates, with each view articulated in a different voice.

In addition to the various outside influences operating on him at this time, certain inner forces exerted themselves to facilitate the division of his poetic vision and channel it into two distinctive voices. One of these forces was his desire to achieve popular and critical acclaim as a major literary figure. This manifests itself most tellingly through his lifelong quest for notoriety. Because he believed that fame could be achieved by drawing attention to himself, his desire for success catalyzed with a certain amount of simple exhibitionism and produced a series of dramatic gestures and outrageous actions. By criticizing individuals, their writing and their beliefs, and by attacking institutions, both civil and religious, he carried this quest for notoriety over into his writing. These assaults grew proportionately more intense as the early novelty of his ploughman-poet image waned.

Another force at work was his natural impulse to speak out about those aspects of Irish life, now particularly Dublin life, that offended him. He compensated for his difficulties in finding steady employment, for instance, by turning on acquaintances who were given certain literary jobs he thought he should have had. In reviews and poems he ridiculed and satirized their work. He also attacked various Dublin attitudes and mores which offended him. Just as he had spoken out against conditions in rural Ireland, he now addressed himself to the task of exposing what he believed were the dehumanizing elements of city life. But of all the pressures that had built up inside him the strongest was his growing sense of alienation. In time it influenced nearly all of his literary work, both critical and creative, and served as the most distinguishing mark of the material he wrote between 1942 and 1955.

This theme of alienation that dominates his middle period began to emerge early in his poetic apprenticeship when he realized that his consuming interest in reading and writing set him apart from his family and neighbors. At first, he romanticized that he was different—that he was a poet. But as this belief grew it became one of the more serious themes of his early poetry and served as the counter to much of the light, comic humor that characterizes *The Green Fool*. Finally, believing that he could not achieve his full potential as a writer in Inniskeen because of its restrictive influences, he settled in Dublin with the hope of joining other writers and becoming part of their artistic world.

Not long after he settled in the city he realized that the stimulating environment he had imagined was little different from the petty and ignorant world he had left. He soon saw through the literary masks many Dublin writers wore to affect an air of artistic sophistication. To him such men were dandies, journalists, and civil servants playing at art. His disgust was deepened by the fact that he was treated as the literate peasant he had been rather than as the highly talented poet he believed he was in the process of becoming. Other factors, such as his lack of education and his ignorance of urban customs and manners, contributed to his ever-growing sense of alienation. The poverty he suffered due to his inability to find steady work also had its effect on him. By the time he had published *The Great Hunger* he had come to believe that in many ways Dublin was as alien a poetic environment as Inniskeen had been. London, he thought, was the one place where a poet could be intellectually at home, but he was uncomfortable there and the war provided a reasonable excuse for not leaving Dublin. For this and other reasons he remained in Ireland and concentrated on extending the limits of his poetic vision by attacking his rivals and peering deeper into his own soul.

II *Fiction*

After Kavanagh published *The Green Fool* in 1938 he began to write "Stony Grey Soil," a precursor of his novel *Tarry Flynn*. The manuscript presents the exploits of a young Irish lad from a northern county who joins a group of friends in an attempt to establish a community hall where they and other local youths can meet and entertain themselves. The young people quickly encounter the wrath of the old parish priest who rules the village absolutely and, fearing for their souls, refuses to sanction the anti-Christ hall, as he calls it. In the course of the action the youthful hero falls in love with the county's most beautiful girl, fails to win her due to the lack of a proper place to woo her, and sees her seduced by a local villain who then abandons her. The hero finally marries a rich though ugly neighbor and settles down to a life of comfort and boredom, using the vacant community hall as a cattle shed.

Kavanagh rewrote "Stony Grey Soil" a number of times and finally sent it to a publisher in London in the spring of 1942. It was quickly returned. Five years passed before he devoted any serious energy to reworking the manuscript. During the spring and summer of 1947 he carried out a series of lengthy revisions. He changed the plot, removing all the material about the village hall, and limited the number of characters. He added a great deal of autobiographical information and retitled the novel "Tarry Flynn." He was aided in his work by Peadar O'Donnell, then editor of *The Bell*, who met with him in a Dublin coffee house several days a week. As Kavanagh finished revising sections of his manuscript, O'Donnell published selections from them in *The Bell* under the title "Four Picturizations." About a year later, after contacting several publishers, Kavanagh sold the book to the Pilot Press, a small London firm who agreed to publish it before the end of 1948. Kavanagh and O'Donnell had hoped that by serializing portions of *Tarry Flynn* in *The Bell* it would pass the Irish Censorship Board once it appeared in hard covers. Unfortunately, this did not prove to be the case; the novel was banned for several months following its appearance in November, 1948.

   Tarry Flynn is essentially a traditional novel. It contains little experimental writing and the plot, though subordinate to character, follows a chronological sequence. The story begins in June, 1935, with Tarry Flynn in his twenty-seventh year, and concludes in the late autumn, with Tarry's decision to leave home. Most of the story, which centers on how he comes to his decision, is told from Tarry's point of view to emphasize his personality and to establish the barriers that isolate him from his family and local community. Tarry is a misfit, though a poetic one, and his sensitivity to the possibilities of life dominates the book and gives it its vitality. He is, Kavanagh would have the reader believe, the only member of his community who has a chance for a fulfilling existence because he alone perceives the richness of life beyond clayey fields and parish church. Of course, Tarry does not fully understand either the meaning or the value of this special insight until the last chapter of the book. Thus, each of the novel's eight chapters present stages of Tarry's blooming awareness, of his initiation into the role of poet and seer.

   Despite its occasional lapses into maudlin romanticism, such as Tarry's departure from his mother at the end of the novel, *Tarry Flynn* is an interesting and, in certain ways, a significant novel. Kavanagh's claim, for instance, that his book is "not only the best but the only authentic account of life as it was lived in Ireland this century" is justified in view of the wealth of realistic detail, activity, and language.[1] In fact, *Tarry Flynn*, if nothing else, is a valuable work of documentary realism. In no other Irish novel, past or present, is the reader offered such an authentic view of daily peasant life. The opening scene is typical. Late for Mass, Tarry searches for a misplaced cap while his mother, suffering from a painful corn on her little toe, lashes out at him for his tardiness. What makes the scene so realistic, what lifts it above the description of other rural fiction is the attention to detail. Tarry nearly steps on some chickens resting near a dresser in one corner of the kitchen as he searches for his cap. All the while his mother keeps at him, complaining: "Hens not fed, the pot not on for the pigs—and you washed your face in the well water" (p. 8). The rest of the scene, the daughter Mary descending the stairs with the night's slops bucket, the mother stirring up the fire and putting on the kettle, and the other daughter, Birdie, moving about the kitchen and tossing remarks about what cow "is looking the bull" and who is involved in the latest local scandal, establishes the human perspective from which the book will develop. Here, then, in terms of locale, the reader is offered a vision of the real rural Ireland rather than the imagined. The novel sustains this authenticity of background as the narrative proceeds through a parish mission, a ritual match-making, a local law suit, and a dozen other common country activities.

Throughout *Tarry Flynn* realism is enhanced by Kavanagh's attention to language. Consider this snip of conversation between Tarry and his friend Eusebius:

> "Hello," Tarry said as he slowed down . . .
> "Damn nice morning," said Eusebius.
> "A terror," said Tarry.
> "Well?" said Eusebius with meaning.
> "Damn to the thing doing, Eusebius," said Tarry.
> "Be jabus! did you see her?"
> "I did. She has no fella as far as I know." (p. 15)

or this bit of verbal jousting between Birdie and her mother:

"Go lang, ye scut, ye," said the mother, "how dar ye say a thing like that to me."

"Oh nobody can talk to you," said Birdie with a pout, "if a person only opens their mouth ye ait the face off them."

"The devil thank ye and thump ye, Birdie, ye whipster, ye. Your face is scrubbed often enough and the damn to the much you're making of it. I could be twice married when I was your age."

"A wonder ye didn't make a better bargain."

"Arra what?" the mother was rising in her anger . . .

This is no stage-Irish dialect. At times Kavanagh's dialogue is so accurate that the non-Irish reader is often hard put to figure out what
is being said. This faithful portrayal of peasant speech not only
provides much of the book's liveliness, but also sustains its authenticity and distinguishes the personalities of the characters.

Mixed in with this documentary realism is a considerable amount
of autobiographical data, and here the novel seems on less certain
ground. To a degree *Tarry Flynn* is a fictional account of certain
sections of *The Green Fool*. In fact, the novel is more
autobiographical in terms of fact and mood than most of *The Green
Fool*. However, despite its local realism, *Tarry Flynn* lacks the verve
and the autobiographical honesty of the earlier book. The reason for
this may lie in the fact that *The Green Fool* illuminates the reality
of Kavanagh's youthful struggle with his talent and his environment
through a series of fabricated circumstances, whereas *Tarry Flynn*
uses thinly disguised actuality as a prism to view romance. In other
words, *Tarry Flynn* presents a view of Kavanagh's life during the
early 1930s not as it was but as he thought it should be if someone
other than himself had lived it. A good example of this is the conclusion he concocted for the book. Pressured between a need for
security and the reassurance familiarity provides on the one hand,
and a desire to escape the confines of rural Ireland on the other,
Tarry Flynn (whom Kavanagh would have the reader believe is
himself at age twenty-seven) flees Dargan with a vagabond uncle to
find fortune and fame in the world beyond. This sounds rather
juvenile, and to an extent it is. It is also far from the real circumstances of his own decision to leave Inniskeen for Dublin.

After *Tarry Flynn* was completed, Kavanagh decided to write
another novel. This unpublished book also depicts rural life as
Kavanagh experienced it. Based upon a short story he had written a
year earlier called "The Cobblers and the Football Team," the
novel has a broader scope than *Tarry Flynn* and features several
main characters.[2] The plot revolves around a group of youthful
cobblers and their antics on the football field. Inniskeen, which is
disguised as Dargan in *Tarry Flynn*, appears as Ballyrush, and the
Inniskeen Rovers Football Club makes its appearance as the
Ballyrush Boggums. Much of the action takes place in Barney
Conlon's small shop. As it was in Kavanagh's own home, people
continually wander in and out of Conlon's kitchen-workroom,
where schemes are hatched, gossip is exchanged, and feuds are
carried on. Although Kavanagh worked at this novel for more than

five years, he never polished it into publishable form. Despite his efforts he could never seem to fit the parts together in any cohesive manner. He finally abandoned the manuscript in the early 1950s when he had other matters to contend with. He did publish part of this uncompleted work, however, in *The Bell* in August, 1951, under the title "Three Pieces from a Novel."

In addition to his two novels, Kavanagh wrote several short stories during the period 1946 - 47.[3] None of them are very remarkable, though they reveal his state of mind during the mid-1940s. Perhaps the two most interesting are "Stars in Muddy Puddles" and "The Lay of the Crooked Knight." Both stories present a theme common to Kavanagh's short fiction of the period. In each case the hero is a highly sensitive man who is treated to a strong dose of unrequited love. In "Stars in Muddy Puddles" the hero is an aspiring writer who is strongly attracted to a young, would-be actress named Mary. While she feels some passion for him—they have a brief affair—she throws him over for a more popular and influential writer, whom she eventually marries in the hope of advancing her career. Mary is shocked back to reality and to the selfishness of her motives when a popular Hollywood film star visits Dublin in search of her former lover. It seems that while she was busy pursuing her career, her abandoned lover had scored successes with his scripts in the film capitals of England and America. The story concludes with Mary disillusioned and her former lover off to Hollywood.

"The Lay of the Crooked Knight," the better of the two stories, attempts a slightly more serious twist to the theme of unrequited love. In this tale the hero is "a crooked knight" who is momentarily distracted from his crusade against the infidels of "Untruth and Charlatanism" by a comely lass who attempts to straighten him out. Because he is in love with her he allows her to smooth out the roughness of his speech and manners. This, the story suggests, is terrible because it weakens his ability and resolve to carry out his sorties against the enemies of culture. Fortunately, all ends well, for the knight discovers that his lover is unfaithful and the shock restores all of his crookedness. Like "Stars in Muddy Puddles," "The Lay of the Crooked Knight" is highly romantic if not downright silly. Kavanagh may have intended these pieces as satires of popular Irish fiction. If he did, they fail in their attempt because he identifies himself too closely with his heroes. The detachment that satire requires is simply missing, with the result that in place of wit balanced with criticism there is nothing but sarcasm. It is more likely that he wrote these stories simply for financial reasons. Whatever the case, they do not contribute much to his literary reputation.

III *Literary and Cultural Criticism*

Kavanagh's first published criticism appeared in the late 1930s. Though his earliest pieces are cautious, the basic approach and peculiar jargon that characterize his later proclamations about literature, its purpose, practice, and functions, are present in his apprentice reviews. Commenting in 1939 on *The Year's Best Poetry: 1938*, for example, he complains in true Kavanaghesque that "some synthetic prophecy is included and some appalling bunk."[4] Six years later both his critical voice and his opinion of Irish poetry had hardened. When he was asked by *The Standard* to survey the achievements of Irish writers during the past fifty years, his remarks about most of his contemporaries were not at all favorable. Focusing on several familiar targets, he wrote that W. R. Rogers "has little to say"; that F. R. Higgins's poetry suffers from "a queer native quality" which makes it "a bit artificial"; that Donagh MacDonagh "is a true poet, but he has read too much and the influences of other poets keep coming through"; and that his old foes, Robert Farren and Austin Clarke, are "much too preoccupied with forms, while their subject matter is rather thin."[5] By the end of the decade these impressions of his fellow poets became even more negative. Writing in the July, 1951, number of *Envoy*, he states quite bluntly that "with the exception of Yeats's work practically none of the verse which was written in Ireland during the past century has had any poetic merit."[6]

The changes that occurred in Kavanagh's critical appraisals during the period 1939 - 52 were brought about more by the expression of his own personal image and particular creative ideals than by the development of objective, critical standards. Impulsive and egotistical, when he examined either life or literature he tended to communicate his creative intensity rather than to detail his intellectual response. As a result, when he turned his energies to criticism he often overreacted, declaring absolutes and making generalizations which satisfied his artistic passion but confused his critical position. To a large extent, this feature of his approach to life and literature contributed to the power of his more successful poems but prevented him from constructing a logical and orderly critical system.

Kavanagh explained his approach and defended his ideals on numerous occasions. Writing in the *Irish Times* in the summer of 1942 he observed that

Some readers may say that I am being romantic. But the romantic attitude is only another name for old decency. And the romantic is the man who is not afraid to speak his mind in praise or condemnation, whereas the 'scholar' and tourist are always waiting to hear what the other fellow says till they steal it to put in the purse of death with the smelly dust.[7]

The image he created for himself, that of the crusading journalist intent on exposing the false and the sentimental, was born of this essentially romantic approach as Kavanagh defined it and was nurtured by a shrewd determination to enforce respect by attack and to exploit the publicity that attack commands. Perhaps the clearest expression of this personal image is contained in "The Lay of the Crooked Knight." In this short piece about the influence of love on the artist, he casts himself as a "Crooked Knight" who

. . . had always had a vocation—to fight against the infidels, Untruth and Charlatanism—to create a great estate, and build a fine castle in place of his present habitation. That done, he would then set to work to express his poetic soul.[8]

In conducting his crusade, the one intention that remains constant and continually emerges from his forays against the "infidels" is the desire to establish an intelligent audience by preaching creative ideals. This audience would be a group of sensitive, perceptive readers who would respond to the needs and ideas of writers and be capable of providing them with encouragement, criticism, and money. Indeed, perhaps the only way to examine Kavanagh's critical writing is to approach it as a body of instruction to educate a select public in the theory and practice of literature.

The beliefs that "the poet is the voice of the people" and that "it is the pressure of people's need for a voice which is [the poet's] power" were expressed with great frequency throughout his apprenticeship and later periods.[9] He devoted nearly the whole of the final number of *Kavanagh's Weekly*, for example, to stressing the writer's need for an audience and the audience's need for literary enlightenment. In fact, he began his weekly newspaper in 1952 because he thought that "every organ of opinion in Ireland [was] in the hands of the enemies of the imagination"[10] and saw as his duty the task of providing a counter-force. When his newspaper failed he retreated to London, complaining that there was no literate audience and no desire in Ireland to create such an audience. However, upon his return to Dublin a year later he changed his mind and announced that

> there does exist in this country a public which accepts all I have to say, a public which has goodwill and a sincere moral point of view. The fact that I believe there is such a public is the reason I am saying these things; for we can only preach to the converted.[11]

Kavanagh believed this audience existed because he believed he had created it by the numerous lessons he had preached through his reviews, articles, columns, stories, and poems during the past fifteen years.

The method of instruction he evolved to create his audience was born of his view of the quiet reading public, as he called them, who were members of the middle class and who resided, for the most part, in the cities. A common mistake made by editors and publishers, according to Kavanagh's analysis, was the "notion that . . . the plain people are suspicious of education, especially when it comes through the medium of writing."[12] Because of this he held that "the idea has been in newspapers and magazines to conceal any sentiments one may have about the value of poetry or similar subjects."[13] To overcome such notions and to correct what he considered an improper approach to creative and critical expression he emphasized rather than concealed his "sentiments" about the various topics he chose to examine. As a result, his zeal to declare himself combined with his desire to educate his readers to produce a strident note of didacticism in much of his writing during these middle years. Thus, it is not surprising that his ideas, particularly about literature, not only dominate his book and film reviews, but also form a rather broad and often loosely ordered literary catechism.

Generally, his catechetical instruction is devoted to three major subjects: the nature of literary (or poetic) art, the function of the poet, and the purpose of criticism. In turn, each subject is divided into specific topics. For example, the nature of literary art includes such items as the definition of poetic art, its value and purpose, and the proper subject matter of poetry. The instruction on the poet's function details various qualities that distinguish the artist from the artificer, with particular attention to the manner in which the poet practices his art. Finally, to provide his readers with proper critical principles, he lectures them about such matters as theme, language, and subject matter, and explains how each should be evaluated.

At the heart of Kavanagh's literary catechism is the twofold doctrine that "no man can be happy who is not in sympathy with the poetic spirit" and that "no society can prosper without the poet's spirit of adventure and courage."[14] To demonstrate the truth of this, Kavanagh directs his energies into an extended and sometimes muddled statement of what poetry is. Writing about Dublin cinema offerings, he interjects some comments about poetry and notes that

> In talking about poetry I may point out that I am not referring to versification or to the verbiage, unfelt, unexperienced, which sometimes nowadays is considered poetry. I am thinking of *the quintessence of experience,** so gay, so full of hope and faith that lives at the heart of things, and which is given expression by all true poets.[15]

To understand the "quintessence of experience" should be the goal of an audience interested in art and Kavanagh never ceases mentioning and discussing it in his critical writing. In another film review he seeks to clarify the matter by explaining that "art is a by-product of truth." He points out that art "is the excitement of seeing things as God sees them—a flower, or a hill or a man, revealed as the miracles they are" and that "no real artist is ever interested in art; he simply tells the truth."[16] Since poetry is art, truth must be the raw material from which the poet extracts the quintessence of experience.

By the early 1950s Kavanagh frequently stressed his belief that poetry is the most serious form of artistic expression. He held that "poetry is not an art only, but something more, a philosophy, a statement of life, a religion."[17] Its attraction, like the attraction of other artistic forms, lies in its power (he explains in *Kavanagh's Weekly*) to enlighten man about himself and about other people in relation to that self. Poetry, like religion, is a way of looking at life, of seeing into the very heart of man's existence. That Kavanagh should choose religion as the metaphor to explain poetry suggests the passion, the emotion, and the intensity of his commitment to it and to establishing a literate, critical audience in Ireland who would foster and participate in its practice.

The process of illuminating the quintessence of experience, of presenting truth, consists of exploding the atoms of ordinary experience, as Kavanagh terms it in one of his monthly *Envoy* diaries. Such detonations enable the poet to take various drab, inconsequential aspects of life and, by charging them with the energy of creative imagination, work a transformation so that their real properties are exposed to the sensitive viewer. Creating poetry, then, involves the proper application of the poet's talent to certain kinds of phenomena and experience in certain specific ways. Kavanagh devotes many of the lessons in his literary catechism to identifying the proper approach. In his essay on F. R. Higgins, for example, he warns that the serious writer should always be on guard against the temptation to manufacture literature from synthetic material. To submit to this temptation is to prostitute one's talent by pandering to an insensitive audience in exchange for public acclaim or financial gain. This is the charge Kavanagh brings against Frank O'Connor in "Colored Balloons." Citing Anton Chekhov as an example of a writer who refused to compromise his talent, Kavanagh explains that Chekhov's genius was marked by "the cutting edge of sincerity ruthlessly piercing through the crust of the ordinary."[18] A true artist never allows himself to be reduced to the artificer's practice of dealing in mere appearances, nor does he embrace the journalist's interest in simply providing entertainment.

To clarify the distinction between proper and improper subject matter Kavanagh often listed subjects that true literary artists ignore. In "Gut Yer Man" (*Envoy*, August 1950) he stated that all sporting material is to be avoided because it is superficial. Another unsuitable subject is nationalism. Its use as a source for poetry sent Kavanagh into rages of high passion. While he spoke out against it during his middle and later periods, it was during the late 1940s, when his criticism of the writers of the Irish Literary Revival reached its greatest intensity, that he gave nationalism its most serious scathing as improper subject matter for literature. Like athletics, the fault with nationalism is its superficiality; it deals with localized appearances rather than with universal reality. To Kavanagh, F. R. Higgins's poetry is superficial in this way. As he explains in "The Gallivanting Poet,"

Higgins grew up in an Ireland which had only recently been invented. There were cheering revivalists (of what we cannot say) and a general bedlam going on which gave everyone the notion that great spiritual activity was in the air. It was like the old charlatan Sequa who used to go around the country curing people of their rheumatism. The patient was brought into a tent where a band was blaring and there he was rubbed and shouted at till he forgot his pain. Home he went without his crutches only to find that the cold of the journey home had revived his rheumatism. That is what happened to us. On the hysteria of nationalistic charlatanism we can shout away our pain no longer. We must dig. Many Irish writers came into being on the wings of this hysteria but when the day of reckoning came they were found without a penny in their pockets, the pennies of experience.[19]

Of course, Higgins was not the only poet whose pockets remained empty. Any writer who uses or implies the use of Irish as the descriptive term for his writing is, in Kavanagh's mind, a nationalistic charlatan. Reviewing Frank O'Connor's *Irish Miles* in the September, 1947, issue of *The Bell,* Kavanagh criticizes O'Connor's comments about certain Irish localities, not because they are untrue but because they offer superficiality in place of genuine artistic vision. In Kavanagh's opinion, O'Connor's quest for Irishness in his travels around Ireland blinded him to the real lessons that can be learned from a survey of the Irish countryside. O'Connor's failure in the book is the failure any writer suffers who is afflicted with the shortsightedness of nationalism. It is, Kavanagh maintained, the "desire to find differences—fantastic people in strange lands—the same childish outlook which speaks of a Kerryman or of a Corkman with some awe as though he were a distinct species" that impairs a writer's vision.[20] The true artist, because he does not let this desire take hold of him, is capable of looking deeply into whatever he chooses to examine and thus sees "the really strange lands and fantastic people that are to be found in the individual commonplace soul."[21]

Kavanagh's criticism of O'Connor is in many ways similar to his criticism of such writers as F. R. Higgins, Austin Clarke, and Robert Farren in that he views their work too subjectively. Often he does not admit the possibility of creative visions other than his own. Because of this, though many of his generalizations about Irish literature are valid, he frequently suffers a critical blindness when he attempts to judge specific contemporary works. His harsh remarks about O'Connor's *Irish Miles,* for example, are unfair when it is remembered that O'Connor was writing a guide book, not an exegesis of the Irish countryside. Also in assessing much of Clarke's poetry, Kavanagh fails to appreciate Clarke's experiments with subject and form because they differ from his own. This rather narrow point of view, occasioned in part by Kavanagh's lack of literary training, was reinforced by his strong creative instincts and his egotism.

In formulating his own poetics, Kavanagh considered the close link between subject matter and purpose the major factor in determining the degree of success a writer achieved. The Literary Revivalists, those writers who were influenced by Yeats's style and themes in their attempts to portray specific aspects of Irish life, were not successful because their purpose, according to Kavanagh, was to recreate something that never existed. When they hunted for unique Irish qualities to give reality to their illusion, they wasted their creative energies and stunted their artistic growth. This is why Kavanagh characterized Higgins's poetry as "a labyrinth that leads nowhere." For similar reasons he criticized the work of Clarke and Farren. To him their poetry lacked substance because they were much too preoccupied with form. He summarized his view of writers who mistakenly concentrate on perfecting form and language rather than on clarifying the quintessence of experience when he wrote that:

A poet can make language an end in itself as some people make sex an end in itself. A little of this decadent point of view has a stimulating effect on literature just as it has in real life. To be completely free from decadence is to be completely dead; but an ideal, a purpose, must be knocking around somewhere if the end is not the utter dissolution, the empty hysteria of *Finnegans Wake*.[22]

There must be a purpose, an ideal, that guides the poet's creative vision past the superficial to the kind of subject matter that will enable his writing to have permanence and value.

To Kavanagh this ideal purpose was the expression of truth. He believed that a poet who pursues truth will eventually discover proper subject matter. Attempting to explain this theory proved difficult for Kavanagh because his lack of disciplined thinking and his penchant for overstating an issue confused many of his readers. A case in point is "Colored Balloons," which provoked some heated discussion first in *The Bell* and later during Kavanagh's unfortunate libel action against *The Leader*. At the center of the controversy was Kavanagh's comment that Frank O'Connor's writing suffers from

. . . a serious defect which can, I think, be attributed to the influence of Yeats . . . a pose of swift indifference to the common earth.

How often as I read did I wish that the author could have thrown in a few spadefuls of the earth's healthy reality — roots, stones, worms, dung. In this patch intelligence could grow.[23]

What Kavanagh meant by this was that a writer should not neglect the reality of his surroundings; he should not neglect those common experiences, places, and events that may serve as valuable subjects for his creative imagination. Most of his critics and many of his friends misinterpreted his remarks in "Colored Balloons" and thought that he was literally arguing for poems and stories full of dung, pitchforks, and chickens in the kitchen.[24] Kavanagh's response was delivered in "Poetry in Ireland ToDay." He explained that "what I seek and love when I find [it] is the whiskey of the imagination, not the bread and butter of 'reality.' This is the thing I seek in writing . . . ."[25] While the distinction here may have escaped some of his contemporaries, to Kavanagh it was quite clear. The flat reality of common earth was not literature. Merely decorating a story or a poem with stones, trees, and clayey soil would not necessarily make it more meaningful. However, the impact that real things such as these make on the imagination could be converted into literature by creative energy. In the process of charging ordinary events, people, places, or objects with the creative imagination a conversion takes place which makes them permanent and potent. This distillation of reality into truth is "the whiskey of the imagination." It is not the reality itself, but what the imagination is capable of doing to it that excited Kavanagh.

Despite his opposition to nationalism and the use of Irish eccentricity as literary materials, Kavanagh believed that it was not only reasonable but also fitting for Irish poets to write about Irish subjects and themes. Indeed, the high praise he has for such different authors as William Carleton and James Joyce springs from their authenticity in treating the reality of Irish life. Their greatness stems from their ability to portray a universal truth by treating specific Irish experiences. Kavanagh emphasized this frequently in his monthly *Envoy* "Diary." In the September, 1950, number of *Envoy*, for example, he noted that "although I have argued that there is no such thing as an Irish mind . . . there are things which have a local individuality; and some hint of this local landscape [in a writer's work] would help to establish [its] genuineness."[26] Irish writers should not be blind to their surroundings. If they want to raise the quality of their writing they should write about what they know best. Mimicking Yeats, Kavanagh wrote:

> Irish poets open your eyes
> Even Cabra can surprise;

> Try the dog tracks now and then—
> Shelbourne Park and crooked men.
> Learn repose on Boredom's bed,
> Deep, anonymous, unread
> And the god of Literature
> Will touch a moment to endure.

Mixed into this theorizing about the nature of poetry is his discussion of the poet. In one of his early reviews in the *Irish Times* he attempted to clarify the essential difference between the artist and the artificer:

What is an artist? Can a writer of best-sellers . . . be an artist? According to one definition, an artist is one who specializes in new ways of saying nothing. He is more interested in the conveyance than in the thing to be conveyed. Usually he has nothing to convey except his own virtuosity . . . This sort of artist is like a ploughman who has horses and plough, but no land. Not being troubled by the urgency of spring sowing he has time to speculate on new theories of ploughing and in this way he is often very useful. [27]

Despite his usefulness, the landless ploughman is not a true artist because his artistry is really artifice: a virtuosity of language and form that dazzles but communicates nothing. A true artist communicates an enthusiasm for life by drawing attention to the wonders of common, ordinary things and the truths they reveal.

Based on this distinction between the artist and the artificer, Kavanagh divided poets into three categories: those who please the critics and stimulate their authentic but sluggish contemporaries; those who lack verbal excitement but who present serious subject matter; and those who combine verbal excitement with serious subject matter. Most of Kavanagh's criticism of the creative writer is directed toward clarifying the basic differences between these three categories of poets. Frequently he devotes himself to ridiculing and exposing the faults, as he sees them, of the first category, the artificers. "The Gallivanting Poet" is typical of these attacks. In other essays and reviews he applauds the achievements of those poets who make real contributions to modern literature. Generally, from his early reviews in the *Irish Times* to his later articles in *Kavanagh's Weekly,* he outlines those specific qualities that mark the genuine creative artist so that his readers will recognize a poet when they see one.

The foremost quality of the poet is creativity, which Kavanagh defined as

the sort of drug produced by the fusion, in a peculiar way, of ordinary things and events. The poet is born-not-made to the extent that no one by taking thought can produce in himself this synthesizing nature . . . The great poets are those who burn in the smithy of their souls the raw material of life and produce from it this erotic-creative essence.[28]

If a poet possessed this power to synthesize the raw materials of life it would be clearly evident in his writing. One indicator of its presence would be the sincerity of his effort. If he gave himself completely to his work and exhibited honesty in his treatment of human experience, it was very likely that he possessed genuine creativity. A poet like F. R. Higgins, Kavanagh believed, lacked sincerity because he refused to see, or was unable to see, the truth in the subjects he chose to write about. Another sign of creativity is the presence of "a transcendent purpose" in an artist's work. "A poet must be going somewhere," Kavanagh explained in "The Gallivanting Poet"; "he must be vitalizing the spirit of man in some way."[29] And, of course, the only true manner in which the poet could accomplish this vitalizing process was by producing the erotic-creative essence.

Ascertaining the presence or absence of creativity was one way of distinguishing between the artist and the artificer. When this "drug" was present, the degree of its potency marked both the category of the poet and the specific value of his poem. Since the artificer was incapable of producing the vital essence, the reader who sought literary enlightenment should limit his search to the work of those writers who were sincere and who possessed creativity. Thus he would be assured of encountering poems that offered him not only a meaningful view of his own habitation, but also the highest of poetic rewards, a sense of spiritual and intellectual growth.

The third subject of Kavanagh's catechetical instruction is the purpose of criticism. In the belief that an intelligent and perceptive audience needed training in the practice of criticism to utilize the lessons it was receiving about poetry and poets, Kavanagh explained the basic principles of critical analysis. Though he occasionally mentioned the critic's duties in his early reviews in the *Irish Times*, it was in his "Round the Cinemas" column in *The Standard* between 1946 and 1947 that he laid down a specific critical code:

(1) To have an attitude, a bias, for as some writer has said, "scales which are evenly held may contain nothing."
(2) To provide readers with a point of view, a point of attack, from which they can proceed to their own judgments.
(3) To see to it that people are thrilled by truth and beauty, not decide what a depraved taste may enjoy.
(4) To be in the fullness of his function not merely public guide but also guide to the artist, writer, or film maker.[30]

These are the critic's primary functions. If he does more or less he is either overstepping the bounds of criticism or failing to meet its minimum requirements. The good critic strikes a balance: on the one hand he presents his own attitude and emphasizes his own point of view, on the other he provides his readers with an objective statement that will aid them in rendering their own judgment. In the process of striking this balance the critic should attempt to direct his readers toward an appreciation of the beauty and value of true art.

How successful Kavanagh was in following his own criteria is questionable. While he did achieve moments of shrewd critical insight in some of his reviews and essays, and while he succeeded in establishing a consistent critical attitude toward literature, his creative passion frequently made it impossible for him to strike a controlled critical balance in his writing. His failure to balance his subjectivity against the objective stance he thought a good critic should adopt is borne out by an examination of what he called for in critical analysis and what he actually did in his own criticism. For example, he warned his readers about the dangers of critics given to extremes in their analysis: those commentators who continually praise or condemn the material they pass judgment on despite its faults or merits. Speaking on this, Kavanagh declared in the August, 1949, number of *Poetry* that "we want some generosity in appraisal, but not the amoral generosity of the journalist to whom all names make news and none poison."[31] A perusal of his critical commentary of this period shows little generosity and much poison. He found very little to be commended in either Irish literature or Irish culture. In fact, his forthcoming *Envoy* diaries would be devoted chiefly to invective against nearly everything that was and had been going on in Ireland since the Literary Revival.

Because he believed that the level of Irish literary achievement was very low, he never ceased stressing his belief that all good criticism was basically destructive. Destruction was necessary because it was the critic's function to save good writing from being submerged in the general flattery of the mediocre. To Kavanagh, the ideal critic was

a sweeping critic who violently hates certain things because they are weeds which choke the fields against the crop which he wants to sow. Truth is personality, and no genuine writer, as a critic, was anything but absolute in his destructiveness.[32]

This stratagem is one Kavanagh often employed in his own criticism. In fact, he so enjoyed matching himself against literary opponents who he thought needed a good critical mauling that he carried the practice over into his poetry. No doubt his verse satires of the 1940s and early 1950s owe their existence to this impulse to swing at those artificers and pseudo-artists who he believed were contributing to the spread of mediocrity in Ireland.

Due to the rather harsh nature of his critical methods, Kavanagh often found himself under attack. In time, as he escalated his war against would-be artists and general mediocrities, his enemies grew in number. While in the earlier stages of his campaign he often took pains to justify his critical barrages, by the time he was publishing *Kavanagh's Weekly* he no longer deemed it necessary to defend his tactics or protect his flanks. Perhaps this was due to the belief that he was fighting from a position near the summit of Parnassus and defending truths that were self-evident. In the early 1940s, however, he often sought to win support for his action against the enemies of literature. He devoted a section of an early review in the *Irish Times* to a lengthy justification of the need for destructive criticism. In noting that a friend had remarked about his destructiveness, Kavanagh commented:

He claimed that blame is easier than praise, which I deny; but that is not really the point. The point is that while, in the abstract, Good always predominates over bad, in this business of books the bad, the fake, and the utterly silly are overwhelmingly in the ascendant.

Because of this, Kavanagh continued:

To use your mind at all is to be critical . . . If a critic is severe, one should find out by what standards and in what perspective the man judges.

He went on to say that his standard was authenticity, "the many-strata truth of imaginative experience."[33] And so he continued delivering his destructive blows whenever he found authenticity wanting until the closing of *Kavanagh's Weekly*, his law suit, and his physical collapse forced a major reexamination of his commitment to poetry.

IV *"Lough Derg"*

The desire to create a perceptive audience was allied with the ever-increasing volume of the public voice in Kavanagh's poetry during the 1940s and early 1950s. Nowhere is this more clearly demonstrated than in "Lough Derg." This long narrative poem, written shortly after *The Great Hunger* and intended to be a sequel to his masterpiece, owes its existence to Kavanagh's concern with presenting a broad analysis of Irish life. Provoked in part by the desire to counter what he saw as the false portrait of Irish life drawn by the Revivalists, and in part by the impulse to continue his investigation of the relationship between his background and himself, "Lough Derg" contains a number of interesting descriptive passages and fine dramatic scenes as well as occasional insights into the spiritual consciousness of troubled pilgrims. Yet it lacks the craft and the control that make *The Great Hunger* a work of literary merit. Perhaps some of the difficulties which flaw "Lough Derg" and which contribute to its failure as a work of major proportion are due to the public voice drowning out the personal voice. The fine balance between objectivity and subjectivity that gives *The Great Hunger* its power and authenticity is not present in this second attempt at a lengthy portrayal of the Irish soul. Instead, the reader is always aware that he is listening to the journalist Kavanagh sermonizing. These lines are typical:

> "And who are you?" said the poet speaking to
> The old Leitrim man.
> He said, "I can tell you
> What I am.
> Servant girls bred my servility:
> When I stoop
> It is my mother's mother mother's mother
> Each one in turn being called in to spread—
> "Wider with your legs" the master of the house said.
> Domestic servants taken back and front.

> That's why I'm servile. It is not the poverty
> Of soil in Leitrim that makes me raise my hat
> To fools with fifty pounds in a paper bank.
> Domestic servants, no one has told
> Their generations as it is, as I
> Show the cowardice of the man whose mothers were whored
> By five generations of capitalist and lord."

The public voice booms too loudly here and there is a false note of contrivance and a heavy-handed didacticism which Kavanagh would later ridicule in the works of his contemporaries. (Much of the poem is closer to the propaganda and the anti-landlordism tracts of the late nineteenth century than to the type of poetry Kavanagh was demanding in his criticism.)

Other sections of "Lough Derg" feature the public voice all too easily commenting on the pathetic state of the pilgrims:

> They come to Lough Derg to fast and pray and beg
> With all the bitterness of nonentities, and the envy
> Of the inarticulate when dealing with the artist.
>
> . . .
>
> Solicitors praying for cushy jobs
> To be County Registrar or Coroner,
> Shopkeepers threatened with sharper rivals
> Than any hook-nosed foreigner.
> Mothers whose daughters are Final Medicals,
> Too heavy-hipped for thinking,
> Wives whose husbands have angina pectoris,
> Wives whose husbands have taken to drinking.

Often the choice of metaphor seems too contrived, as if the poet is forcing his theme and his vision rather than letting it emerge subtly as it does in *The Great Hunger*. Describing the beginning of the second day of the pilgrimage, for example, Kavanagh reports that

> Morning from the hostel windows was like the morning
> In some village street after a dance carouse,
> Debauchees of Venus and Bacchus
> Half-alive stumbling wearily out of a bleary house.
> So these pilgrims stumbled below in the sun
> Out of God's publichouse.

Unlike *The Great Hunger*, which ends with a strong, forceful image, requiring no comment and receiving none from the poet to make its full impact on the reader's imagination, "Lough Derg" closes as it opens, with Kavanagh explaining what his poem should have portrayed:

> All happened on Lough Derg as it is written
> In June nineteen-forty-two
> When the Germans were fighting outside Rostov.
> The poet wrote it down as best he knew
> As integral and completed as the emotion
> Of men and women cloaking a burning emotion
> In the rags of the commonplace, will permit him.
> He too was one of them.

As a sequel to *The Great Hunger* "Lough Derg" is a failure. However, it is not without value as an experiment in exercising the public voice. What it demonstrates quite clearly is the fact that Kavanagh now needed some form other than the long narrative to articulate effectively the complexities of Irish life.

V   *Poems of Art and Artifice*

The presence of the public voice in so much of his poetry indicates the change that had occurred in Kavanagh's thinking regarding the nature and the function of the poet in the years immediately following the publication of *The Great Hunger*. In a short, reflective poem entitled "After Forty Years of Age," he presents his new concept of the poet's duties:

> The job is to answer questions
> Experience. Tell us what life has taught you.
>   Not just about persons—
> Which is futile anyway in the long run—but a
>   concrete, as it were, essence.
>
> The role is that of prophet and saviour. To
>   smelt in passion
> The commonplaces of life. To take over the
>   functions of a god in a new fashion.

It is no longer enough merely to celebrate aspects of your surroundings, voice personal reflections, or muse over past events. Now the poet must establish himself as an interpreter, a practicing seer whose primary duty and chief goal are to inform and teach his readers about the true essence of life and its values. Kavanagh gave himself fully to these duties and wrote a number of poems in which he catalogues the necessary practices and the proper qualities required for a meaningful participation in life. In "A View of God and the Devil," for example, he distinguishes between the ideal ("Amusing/ Experimental/ Irresponsible—/ About frivolous things") and the mediocre ("Solemn,/ Boring,/ Conservative"). The devil is the ultimate mediocrity:

> He was a man the world would appoint to a Board.
> He would be on the list of invitees for a bishop's
>   garden party,
> He would look like an artist.
> He was the fellow who wrote in newspapers about
>   music,
> Got into a rage when someone laughed;
> He was serious about unserious things;
> You had to be careful about his inferiority complex
> For he was conscious of being uncreative.

This distinction provided the basis for a number of poems about individuals who appreciate the true essence of life and those who fail to perceive it.

"Jim Larkin," his eulogy to the famous Irish union organizer, is one of Kavanagh's best efforts to translate that vision into action. He praises Larkin for being more "Than a labour-agitating orator." Larkin directed men, Kavanagh explains, to look about them and see the beauty and the joy that could be theirs if they would only let the vitality that was in them have its way:

> Jim Larkin came along and cried
> The call of Freedom and the call of Pride
> And Slavery crept to its hands and knees
> And Nineteen Thirteen cheered from out the utter
> Degradation of their miseries.

In another poem that might be considered an eulogy, "A Wreath for Tom Moore's Statue," Kavanagh attacks the attitudes and intentions of the insensitive and artless souls who wreathe statues rather than honor living poets. Like "Jim Larkin," this poem is successful because the public voice is kept under control through a shrewd selection of detail. From the poem's opening lines Kavanagh establishes and then sustains an attack without wandering into side issues or sinking into an emotional harangue against the philistines. Though he states that "No poet's honoured when they wreathe this stone," the remark is not meant as a criticism of Moore. A parenthetical note, "Not concerning Thomas Moore," included below the poem's title is no doubt meant as support for this. It is the fitting out of corpses to deceive, as Kavanagh terms it, that has raised his ire. Such worship of stone idols is the philistine's feeble response to art and to life. He lacks the courage to confront truth and, like a coward, hides his fear behind fake ideals and phony gestures. The use of the word "stone" instead of statue or poet throughout the poem underscores this criticism and serves as subtle reminder that what is being honored is not the poet's living work but a cold, lifeless facsimile of his outward appearance. In a larger sense, the poem is also an attack on those writers who, like the philistines, waste their energies treating mere appearances and never force themselves to undertake the difficult task of penetrating through the crust of life to render its true essence in honest works of art.

VI   *Verse Satire*

It was basically due to his concern for the state of Irish culture and to his desire to expose the false and the sham that Kavanagh wrote his satiric poetry of the 1940s and early 1950s. While he expressed his concern with culture and art in a few poems written shortly after his arrival in Dublin, he addressed these efforts to Irish culture in general rather than to specific individuals. The satires and parodies of fellow Irish writers began in earnest during the mid-1940s in the period immediately preceding his *Envoy* diary. Of course, he occasionally assailed friends and foes in his journalism, beginning with his early reviews in the *Irish Times* and in *The Standard*. However, by the late 1940s the public voice in his poetry merged, as it were, with the critical voice of his journalism and produced a series of interesting and highly effective satires of the thinking and writing of popular Irish literary figures.

Two poetic experiments that opened the way for these poems are "On Reading Jack Yeats's New Novel" and "Bardic Dust." The former, which first appeared in the *Irish Times*, is a clever review of

Yeats's *Ah, Well* presented as a Petrarchan sonnet. Evaluating the book, Kavanagh complains:

> I've tried to find in this book of yours, Jack Yeats,
> Some growthy patch sown with the enchanted seed
> Of Grimm or Carroll or Lear—as is the need
> Of children in a world of rent and rates.

He concludes: "But nothing happens here, Jack Yeats, where you/ Have spun your web of childish fantasy." Kavanagh may have chosen to review *Ah, Well* in this way out of boredom with what had become a weekly ritual for him, i.e., the two- to three-hundred word standard newspaper review. In any case, his choice of form for this particular review was not only creative and refreshing, it was also apt and revealing. The use of the highly stylized sonnet was a subtle comment on the excesses in Yeats's prose.

"Bardic Dust" is a review of Austin Clarke's *The Viscount of Blarney and Other Plays* and a witty criticism of Clarke's work as a whole. A parody of verse-drama, "Bardic Dust"'s innovative format allowed Kavanagh to ply freely a sharp critical knife with which to slice up his foe. The playlet opens with the Public chanting in chorus: "We hate verse-plays, we hate verse-plays/ We do not think there are worse plays." Next, Kavanagh himself appears and soliloquizes:

> I shall not give the Public's poison-piety rein.
> And yet I cannot praise,
> Honestly, these ghostly lyric plays.

Clarke enters dressed as a Medieval Abbot. To Kavanagh's comment, "This Clarke is always three removes from life," an Editor replies:

> Be easy, critic, with the butcher's knife,
> For I'll allow no man to say
> That Clarke is not a good poet anyway.

The action continues with Clarke reading some inane lines from *The Viscount of Blarney* and Kavanagh interjecting the remark that

> Poetry
> Is not in scansion, form, rhymes,
> But in the intense gospel of our times.
> Poetry is not something sweetly nice.

Kavanagh suggests that Clarke's main problem, the error that flaws his writing, is his zealous commitment to the mechanics rather than to the substance of poetry. Because he devotes his energies almost solely to the perfection of form, his work is out of balance and he succeeds in creating highly polished but ultimately meaningless verse. He is sweetly nice instead of vitally real. And a poet, Kavanagh informs his reader, should be

> . . . a man twice
> As much alive as any other man;
> His time wounds him more deeply than
> It wounds the common
> Man or woman.

If the essence of life, if the tragedy and the comedy of real human experience is not present in a poet's work, then that work, despite its polish and its craft, has little value.

Like the best of his satiric pieces, "Bardic Dust" is effective because Kavanagh chose to expose his man through parody and satire. The very form of the review, mock-verse drama, provides a direct method of ridiculing Clarke's dramatic talents and his basic approach to poetry. While Kavanagh continued to utilize various verse forms as vehicles for his satiric voice, his most successful attacks on the purveyors of the false and the sham are delivered through innovative presentations like "Bardic Dust." Indeed, such well-directed and sustained thrusts as "The Wake of the Books," "The Paddiad," and "Adventures in the Bohemian Jungle," though different in form and approach, share a common method of treatment based upon intuitive critical insight and a spontaneous response to life and literature which originated in "Bardic Dust."

"The Wake of the Books" is a mummery in rhymed couplets that features a large number of speakers, ranging from prominent writers to young solicitors. Published in the November, 1947, issue of *The Bell*, "The Wake of the Books" was written as a response to Peadar O'Donnell's editorial, "Suggestions For A Fighting Wake," (*The Bell*, July 1947). Though O'Donnell sought some creative effort that would commemorate the passing of the Ministry for Fine

Arts, Kavanagh offered up a humorous blast at what had by now become familiar targets for his critical guns. Wealthy businessmen, film directors, actors, politicians, and certain writers, all take a turn on the mummer's stage and utter some characteristic foolishness about literature and censorship. Kavanagh himself is both the Master of Ceremonies and a member of the cast. While he announces his main theme in the prologue:

> As I lead the characters in I'll try
> To show the kernel of the tragedy—
> The reality of bank and bake-house
> Screeching unheeded round the writers' wake-house,
> The inarticulate envy and the spleen
> Echoing in the incidental scene
> We call the Censorship.

he makes it quite clear in the body of the poem that the problem of censorship itself is not as serious as the pseudo-cultural state of mind that allows it to be practiced. "The Wake of the Books" satirizes the erroneous ideals and the misguided enthusiasm that produces a society where "The horse is mightier than the pen" and "The journalists cheer loudly for all/The noblest verse and stupidest doggerel." In such a society it is no wonder that real intellectual life is dead. As a result, fakery and artistic charlatanism have grown up and become the new gods of a thoughtless public.

It is to Kavanagh's credit that in treating the subject of censorship and the intellectual wasteland in which it thrives he never becomes too didactic. By keeping his creative passion in check and utilizing the best elements of satire, he presents a clever if not altogether accurate appraisal of the Irish literary scene. Though the poem is filled with humor, it ends with the somber comment that the writers who cart off the coffin of waked books are

> . . . living in yesterday.
> Challenging the enemy that died last night
> For the spirit in travail now they have no sight
> To see or ears to hear, or words to name
> The lies that crowd around this day's life-dream.

"The Paddiad: Or the Devil as a Patron of Irish Letters" was written after "The Wake of the Books" and is narrower in scope, focusing on specific Irish writers who devote themselves to the dull and the dead. Intended as a comprehensive satire on those who revel in the trappings of literary art but who lack both the vision and the commitment to explore life honestly, the poem is modeled after Alexander Pope's *Dunciad* and presents Austin Clarke, Robert Farren, and M. J. McManus, among others, as silly, affected literary dilettantes. Set in a typical poets' pub, the piece opens with all the "Paddies,"

> Paddy Whiskey, Rum and Gin
> Paddy Three sheets in the wind;
> Paddy of the Celtic Mist,
> Paddy Connemara West,
> Chestertonian Paddy Frog

"croaking" in their bog. The poem's themes, that these poets are unwilling to see themselves honestly and that they sustain themselves and their reputations at the expense of literature, are brought out by parodying behavior and conversation. Seated in a circle around "The master of the mediocre" they discuss each other's work and praise the teachings of their mentor. Into their midst strides Paddy Conscience, "A man who looks the conventional devil." He disrupts their evening by shouting and roaring the truth at them and they throw him out of the pub. With Conscience gone, they are free to be themselves and assume their pompous poses. The poem ends with all of the Paddies, on hearing the news of Conscience's death, hurrying home to write

>   the inside story
> Of their friendship for the late
> Genius who was surely great;
> Recall his technical innovations,
> His domestic life, his patience
> With humblest aspirant
> On the literary bent.

The "Devil Mediocrity" remains in the pub, sitting alone, discontented in the knowledge that another Conscience will soon appear to harass him and his poetical frogs.

The third lengthy satire Kavanagh wrote during his middle period, "Adventures in the Bohemian Jungle," was published in the April, 1950, number of *Envoy*. Like "Bardic Dust" and "The Wake of the Books," this piece dramatizes specific literary and cultural

faults and weaknesses by treating humorously the responsible personalities and attitudes. While the poem is not as balanced as "The
Wake of the Books" nor as devastating as "The Paddiad," it
employs the same wit and satiric techniques. Unlike the other
poems, "Adventures in the Bohemian Jungle" is more ambitious in
its attempt at rendering the whole social and cultural world of Irish
art as a living hell for the intelligent and the sensitive. Kavanagh
called his sketch "A Play" when it appeared in *Envoy*. However,
"Adventures in a Bohemian Jungle" is no ordinary play. It is a
curious combination of the medieval Morality play and modern Ex-
pressionist drama. The reader follows the adventures of a simple
countryman, "A true believer in the mystical/Power of poets," who
is led through the Bohemian Jungle in a search for art. The scenes
are Dantesque, complete with drunken women, wealthy patrons,
American tourists, zealous clergymen, and assorted hangers-on, all
drawn to "the phallic tower of Bohemia's temple, the Theatre."
Like allegorical figures in a Morality play, the characters are one-
dimensional, physical manifestations of abstract human qualities:
charlatanism, depravity, snobbery, and the like. In place of order,
the Bohemian Jungle presents chaos. The countryman, not surprisingly, is shocked by what he finds. Instead of meeting poets
making poems, he is jostled by politicians carrying flags, women
staggering into bedrooms, and travel guides extolling Irish
fleshpots. His guide tells the innocent countryman to

> See life as newspapers show it
> Without a moral judgement,
> The bank Integrity
> Holds but a beggar's lodgement.
> Truth's what's in power to-day,
> The lie's what's in the breadline
> So take your Gospel straight
> From the morning headline.

As the drama draws to a close, the countryman, perceiving the
superficiality of this world, declares:

> . . . here in this nondescript land
> Everything is secondhand;
> Nothing ardently growing,
> Nothing coming, nothing going,
> Tepid fevers, nothing hot,

Nothing alive enough to rot,
Nothing clearly defined . . .
Every head is challenged.

The grotesque world Kavanagh depicts in this poem represents one of his heaviest barrages at the philistines. He portrays them as individuals gone mad in a cultural hell, men and women pursuing the base pleasures of the emotions instead of seeking the simple truths of the real world and the rich rewards of the mind. In place of the lofty ideals of art they have substituted the facile glitter of artifice.

VII   A Soul for Sale: *The Personal Voice*

The public voice accounts for less than half of the poetry that Kavanagh wrote during the 1940s and early 1950s. Most of the poems in *A Soul for Sale*, for example, are devoted to an illumination of Kavanagh's private concerns. Like much of his apprentice poetry, the book continues his investigation of the self through rural images and pastoral scenes. There are several reasons for this. Kavanagh had spent most of his life in Monaghan and in the surrounding areas, and it was only natural that he should draw upon this experience for his personal poems. Also, Dublin did not appeal to him in the 1940s as suitable subject matter for the personal voice. The desire to build a new habitation for the soul, as he termed it in "The Lay of the Crooked Knight," could not be realized in the turmoil of Dublin life. While Monaghan had not satisfied him, it was not foreign to his poetic soul, and he tended to view it rather nostalgically now that he had left it.

In addition, *A Soul for Sale* offers a view of the private man behind the loud, often offensive public figure. Masked by the rage of the public voice is the personal frustration Kavanagh felt in trying to find his way in Dublin. Indeed, all of his public lessons about literature and criticism are related directly to a desire to arrange his changing ideas about poetry and a need to understand his failure to achieve popular acclaim. While it may be too harsh to say that Kavanagh was suffering a loss of confidence in his talent during these years, there is little doubt that he was very conscious of not achieving the success he had hoped his move to Dublin would bring him. Many of his poems, particularly those published in the early 1950s, are concerned with failure. The very title *A Soul for Sale* suggests the degree to which failure was involved in his self-examination. It is ironic that while the public voice is so strong and confident in its outcries against the philistines, the personal voice is often subdued in its utterances about the state of Kavanagh's own poetic soul.

Kavanagh seemed to be aware of this distinction in his poetry. He touched upon the subject when he noted in "The Gallivanting Poet" that the essential difference between a public and a private speaker is that the former merely reports circumstances while the latter lives them. That Kavanagh lived his failure and his isolation is borne out by *A Soul for Sale*. The poem "Pegasus" characterizes the book and illustrates Kavanagh's view of his personal position during the mid-1940s. Though the poem is rather sentimental, and though Kavanagh later rejected it as mere affectation, it accurately summarizes the sources of his frustration and documents his response to failure. Comparing his soul to an old horse, a rather nagging metaphor, he explains that neither church nor state cared to relieve him of the beast, whereupon it grew wings and, like Pegasus, took flight. The poem seems to have been written out of defiance and acceptance. By proclaiming a victory of the imagination, Kavanagh defies the institutions and the social structures that have denied him the success he has tried so hard to achieve in Dublin. At the same time he accepts his failure in the practical world. Unfortunately, Kavanagh neglects to note the irony that his problems might never have arisen if he had not set popular acclaim and financial reward as the measures of artistic success.

The theme of failure occurs in other poems. At times the pain cannot be so easily written off as it is in "Pegasus." In "The Gift"[34] a rather pathetic portrait of the poet in misery is conveyed when Kavanagh, obviously concerned with his personal image and his loneliness, catalogues his problems and asks for deliverance from them:

> Getting into jeopardy,
> Being savage, wild and proud
> Fighting, arguing with the crowd;
> Being poor, sick, depressed,
> Everywhere an awful pest;
> Being too right, being too wrong,
> Being too weak, being too strong,
> Being every hour fated
> To say the things that make me hated;
> Being a failure in the end—
> God, perfection on me spend.

The forces that were allying against him because of his harsh critical remarks made him feel more isolated. Ironically, the more isolated he became, the more fiercely he struck out at his antagonists. By 1945 he felt quite alone in an alien world. He put his position clearly in "From Failure Up":

> Maybe this is what [man] was born for, this hour
> Of hopelessness . . .
> Where the web of Meaning is broken threads
> And one man looks at another in fear.
> O God can a man find You when he lies with his
>   face downwards
> And his nose in the rubble that was his achievement?
> Is the music playing behind the door of despair?
> O God give us purpose.

Not all of Kavanagh's personal writing of the period is as heavy-hearted as this. In addition to attacking his enemies in his public poems, he also consoled himself in his personal writing by romanticizing many of his difficulties. The most highly romantic and perhaps the most humorous of these pieces are those that focus on his relationships with women. He was, in fact, deep in the throes of affectation with a particular girl from Kerry during the mid-1940s. He glamorized this relationship in the short story "Stars in Muddy Puddles." This piece, and others like it, no matter how sentimental, doubtless served to salve Kavanagh's bruised ego and earn him a few pounds. Indeed, the need to triumph, in fiction if not in fact, lay at the heart of these efforts. However, one of these pieces, the poem "On Raglan Road," is a clever adaptation of a traditional ballad and shows that he could still laugh at himself.

Romanticizing his condition had limited value and it was principally by going back to his creative roots in Inniskeen that Kavanagh sought to understand his failure. In "Temptation in Harvest" he returns to a reconsideration of that decision made in the late 1930s to leave the farm to pursue poetry—the decision that has brought him his misery. The poem begins with the realization of his present failure clearly reflected in his rural surroundings. As he had done so often in his earlier poetry, he mirrors his mental state through a description of nature:

> A poplar leaf was spiked upon a thorn
> Above the hedge like a flag of surrender

> That the year hung out. I was afraid to wonder
> At capitulation in a field of corn.

The beauties and the joys of his country past still have power over him. The first of several temptations now occurs as he surveys an autumn worker making a stick into a farm tool. For the present he feels tempted to throw up the literary trade and move back to the farm. He bemoans his desire to possess creative vision which has brought about his present uncertainty. Yet he rejects this temptation in the knowledge that "Clay could still seduce my heart/ After five years of pavements raised to art." Conscious of the fate of living too close to the soil, the fate of Patrick Maguire, he shouts:

> O the devilry of the fields!
>
>   . . .
>
> Where can I look and not become a lover
> Terrified at each recurring spasm?

Sinking into reverie once more, he reflects on the various duties of the harvest in years past and how he often withstood the temptation that poetry then posed for him. In those years the fields held him firmly. He accepted the idea that "You cannot eat what grows upon Parnassus" and yet he was dazzled by the beauties of poetic vision and remained indecisive as to which choice to make:

> The air was drugged with Egypt. Could I go
> Over the field to the City of the Kings
> Where art, music, letters are the real things?
> The stones of the street, the sheds, hedges cried, No.
> Earth, earth! I dragged my feet off the ground.
> Labourers, animals armed with farm tools,
> Ringed me. The one open gap had larch poles
> Across it now by memory secured and bound.
> The flaggers in the swamp were the reserves
> Waiting to lift their dim nostalgic arms
> The moment I would move. The noise of carts
> Softening into haggards wove new charms.
> The simplest memory plays upon the nerves
> Symphonies that break down what the will asserts.

By clarifying the nature of his old dilemma Kavanagh was able to tap once more the spring that had nourished his imagination and provided him with the courage to choose poetry. In a sense, this poem and others like it became rituals in which he reaffirmed his commitment to his talent and from which he gained strength to accept and eventually overcome his current difficulties.

His search for the self that began with his need to reorient himself in regard to poetry and his relationship to it opened the way for a thorough revaluation of his literary ideals and his creative values. By the early 1950s Kavanagh was writing different kinds of personal poems from those he had written in the mid-1940s. In several poems published in *The Bell* and *Envoy,* such as "Ante-Natal Dream," "The Defeated," and "Epic," the theme of failure gives way to a new concept of the self. This was partly due to the rebirth Kavanagh spoke of in the late forties that was initiated by his work on *Tarry Flynn.* This novel contributed to his search for the self and aided him in reordering priorities because it provided a further opportunity for him to survey his earlier life and portray it authentically. This is not to suggest that *Tarry Flynn* is a completely realistic portrait of the poet as a young man. Indeed, much of the book features the same sort of romantic invention that is present in *The Green Fool.* However, it is a true picture of farm life and of Kavanagh's first struggles with creative vision. He emerged from his work on *Tarry Flynn* with the knowledge that what is important in literature is the truthful treatment of material accompanied by an honest statement of personal vision. He announced this discovery in one of his film reviews in *The Standard:*

The trouble with a novel, or any work of art, is that the theme is often nothing. It is the background, the sensibility, which is the real message. The personality of the writer is the valid part of his theme. It is the ignoring of this fact that the personality is part of a man's statement of truth which invalidates newspaper stories. The journalist is supposed to submerge his own personality and accept amorally the blind facts.[35]

Kavanagh now actively sought to depict his personal vision in such poems as "Kerr's Ass" and "On Looking into E.V. Rieu's Homer." His problem was to understand the self well enough to present a clear portrait of it. In order to do this he experimented with the pastoral poetry he had often written during his apprenticeship. "Innocence," a good example of this type of poem, could easily be mistaken for something out of *Ploughman and Other Poems* because of its situation and subject matter. Like "Shancoduff," "Innocence" is concerned with isolation brought about by

the creative imagination. Explaining that his love for a small hill
makes him appear foolish to his neighbors, he remarks that "They
said/That I was bounded by the whitethorn hedges/Of the little
farm and did not know the world." The poem ends by attempting
to clarify the nature of the poet's existence:

> I know nothing of women,
> Nothing of cities,
> I cannot die
> Unless I walk outside these whitethorn hedges.

While this poem and other experiments with the pastoral mode,
such as "On Reading a Book of Common Wild Flowers," serve as
reflections of the poetic self, they suggest an ideal existence rather
than an authentic statement of his present condition. Because of
this, Kavanagh abandoned these experiments and turned his efforts
to a more realistic appraisal in such poems as "I Had a Future,"
"Auditors In," and "To Be Dead."

These poems attempt honest statements of failure. "To Be Dead"
outlines the ways in which failure is manifested to the poet. The
poem objectively treats the death of the creative impulse, which is
signalled by a loss of belief, a lack of growth, and a retreat to
rationalization and religion. Unlike "To Be Dead," "I Had a
Future" is a lament for what might have been rather than a statement of what has come to pass. Its scope is more personal, a kind of
private confession in which the speaker is painfully aware of his
failure to realize the bright future that once lay before him. There is
an honesty in the poem that is not present in such earlier self-
portraits as "Pegasus" and "Love Is but a Season." Because of this,
the poem's pathos is genuine and the poet's sensibility comes
through clearly, free of contrivance and self-pity. It is in "Auditors
In," however, that the most objective and the most thorough
analysis of the self takes place. The poem begins:

> The problem that confronts me here
> Is to be eloquent yet sincere;
> Let myself rip and not go phony
> In an inflated testimony.

In this desire to appraise the self truthfully he questions "Precisely
how I chanced to fail/Through a cursed ideal." He audits his soul's

account, listing items he sought to purchase with his creativity: a
car, a suburban house, sexual pleasure, and popularity. He tallies
his debits and credits:

> You are not homosexual.
> And yet you live without a wife,
> A most disorganized sort of life.
> You've not even bred illegitimates
> A lonely lecher whom the fates
> By a financial trick castrates.
>
> You're capable of an intense
> Love that is experience.
>
> . . .
>
> Your imagination still enthuses
> Over the dandelions at Willie Hughes'
> And these are equally valid
> For urban epic, a peasant ballad.

and concludes

> It's on your hand, the humble trade
> Of versing that can easily
> Restore your equanimity
> And lay the looney ghosts that goad
> The savages of Pembroke Road . . .
> Bow down here and thank your God.

In the second section of the poem he celebrates the joy of con-
fronting the self honestly and the pleasure of knowing that spiritual
and creative growth is still possible. Admitting past errors has a
cleansing effect and the poem ends with a statement of relief:

> I am so glad
> To come accidentally upon
> My self at the end of the tortuous road
> And have learned with surprise that God
> Unworshipped withers to the Futile One.

This was Kavanagh's mood shortly before his world began to
collapse around him. The personal and the public struggles in
which he had been involved for the last decade were beginning to
subside when he suddenly found himself entangled in new dif-

ficulties. The inner peace he had only recently secured at the expense of personal pride was now threatened by an attack on his professional image. His hasty reaction to the satiric "Profile" of him that appeared in *The Leader* in October, 1952, initiated a series of actions that would result in disillusionment and defeat for him. The closing of *Kavanagh's Weekly* and the retreat to London signalled the end of Kavanagh's middle period. What followed was a lengthy two-year span of psychological pain and physical suffering that served as an unpleasant transition from the personal soul-searching and the public outcries of the 1940s to the rebirth and reassessment of the late 1950s and early 1960s.

CHAPTER 5

Return and Rebirth: 1955 - 1967

I *The Context for Change*

ON a June day in 1924, embarrassed by his family's reaction to some of his earliest poetry, Kavanagh had consoled himself by writing in his personal notebook:

Wisdom from weakness aids you. When we are most foolish that is the time to study our real selves. That is the time to peer into the recesses of our minds and ask the question, 'where is my worth?' I write this because I have played the seer and have been made a fool of by those whom I considered fools.[1]

In a general way, this statement also characterizes Kavanagh's mood during the period that followed his libel action against *The Leader* and his unfortunate illness in 1954. From the winter of 1954 to the spring of 1955 was a time of severe mental and physical pain for him. In fact, he often spoke of it as being the most desolate period of his life. During the long months of his recovery in Dublin, Longford, and Inniskeen, however, he began an honest reassessment of himself and his poetry, seeking to profit from his misfortunate by reordering his personal and literary values.

With this desire to reassess and reevaluate, Kavanagh began the last phase of his literary career. As he had in the past when confronted with personal failure, he reaffirmed his faith in those lifelong critical and creative ideals he believed would sustain and aid him in reorienting his thinking. His public utterances during the late 1950s and early 1960s, for example, continued to stress the poet's need for an intelligent, sympathetic audience and to emphasize nature's value as a source of revelation. To a large extent, nature's hold on him became stronger during this period than it had been in the early years of his apprenticeship. He attributed the rebirth of his creativity and artistic perception to nature's in-

114

fluence. He remained firm, too, in his stand against both the misuse of Irish subjects and themes and the malpractice of criticism. While his remarks about literature, its practice and content, were often less passionate than they had been, they remained consistent with his earlier critical pronouncements. However, he restricted his criticism to his prose and abandoned verse satire almost completely, devoting his creative energies to a renewed quest for the self. Along with familiar pronouncements about the literary shortcomings of his contemporaries, he continued to voice his own creative ideals. Whether he dismissed W. B. Yeats's philosophical systems or John Synge's vision of Irish life, Kavanagh maintained that only a simple, direct statement of common, ordinary experience was the proper response for the poetic artist. Above all, he stressed that poetry was primarily a religious experience, with the poet serving as an artistic theologian. As in the past, this belief was accompanied by a strong faith in the power of the imagination. The poet's primary function remained the sincere expression of the excitement produced by the imagination focusing on specific aspects of everyday life. To Kavanagh, "the true mark of the poet," as he had written nearly ten years earlier, continued to be "the ability to project a particular case into the larger consciousness, to show even the most insignificant event as of universal importance."[2]

In addition to these ideals and beliefs, the isolation that dominates so much of his earlier writing and serves as the theme for so many of his poems continued to influence his response to life and literature. The trial confirmed what he had believed for nearly thirty-five years: that he was essentially alone in a world that had become, over the years, increasingly alien to his artistic position. In both his letters and his poems of the late 1950s and early 1960s the tone of isolation is struck again and again. A survey of his rather nostalgic and light-hearted columns in both the *Irish Farmers' Journal* and the *RTV Guide* clearly shows the frustration he suffered in his search for a spiritual and creative home and confirms the degree to which his sense of being an outsider in both country and city dominated his thinking.

Generally, the last twelve years of Kavanagh's literary career fall into four phases of varying creative intensity. The first period, artistic disorientation, is characterized by the need for personal evaluation and creative assessment. By examining the self and its relationship to poetry the way could be opened for new growth. A period of spiritual rebirth, occasioned by the honest evaluation of the self, lasted some three years and was marked by a resurgence of creative vitality. The period of creative growth that followed his rebirth was marked by numerous attempts to implement the poetic doctrine he summarized as "not caring," which replaced his previous commitment to social awareness. Finally, as his health worsened and as his creative vitality ebbed, he began groping for ideas and his literary efforts diminished.

II   *Evaluation and Redirection*

A brief survey of his post-trial poetry indicates the direction his final development would take. Summing up his position in the short poem "Nineteen Fifty-Four," he complains that his creative energies have been drained from him and that his critical priorities are disturbed and distorted. In the midst of this disorientation, Kavanagh acknowledges the need to reassure himself and to affect an image of confidence so that his enemies, whom he believed were ready to dismiss him as a broken man, would not be aware of the true depths of his suffering. While he was disheartened and, to a degree, embarrassed by the outcome of the libel action against *The Leader,* he never really lost faith in his talent. In other poems, such as "Intimate Parnassus," he sets out the code that would sustain him through his difficulties and from which he would soon draw the energy for a spiritual rebirth: to detach himself from his suffering and see it impersonally as one aspect of the human situation. Because he believed that he could escape his problems only by writing objectively about them, he gave himself to the task of examining the nature of personal failure. In "The Son of God" he treats it as a necessary sacrifice expected from the highly talented and the gifted. Viewing his own position, he explains in the poem that he refuses to be trapped by other men's ideas of suffering.

Personal sacrifice is also the theme of "Inscription for the Tomb of the Unknown Warrior." This poem is not a simple parable about suffering. Unlike "The Son Of God," it presents a poignant portrait of a warrior-poet who seeks to redeem himself through an admission of his faults. Written as a monologue, and with an obvious autobiographical tenor, the poem presents Kavanagh's critical and practical failures with unusual frankness. The title suggests that Kavanagh still pictured himself as a crusading warrior. This romanticism is typical of his lifelong conception of himself and indicates the temptation he felt during his post-trial period to give in to self-pity. Until his rebirth provided a new self-image, he continued to see himself as a defender of art and culture brought low by the enemies of literature. Yet he was not bitter, as the poem's final eight lines indicate:

> Forgive the temper that I seem to show
> In this long aside about my final foe.
> He said a pea-size thought would burst my gizzard—
> I ultimately perished in his blizzard.
> All that I did while posing as a man
> Was dictated by a eunuch's bitter plan.
> But I am dead, pray God that so I stay,
> And Dublin free to be sincere and gay.

In satirizing his defeat and attributing his errant behavior to "a eunuch's bitter plan," the humor that vitalizes so much of his criticism of the 1940s emerges here and enables him to overcome the temptation to wallow in self-pity. Even in defeat Kavanagh manages to admit his faults and laugh at himself and his enemies.

Other post-trial poems, however, indicate that he was not always able to detach himself from his subject matter. In "Failure of a Kind" he speaks less objectively about his personal pain:

> . . . sometimes I feel I've about had it, arsing
> Around among the ever-rising antes,
> Small-time auctioneers standing nattily
> Up at the gleaming bar holding on to a gin,
> Policemen's sons who've made it glance around at me[.]
>   . . .
> They cannot see my mind gyrating wittily
> Compassionate me gagging my laughter's sin.

His frustration comes from an unsureness, the disorientation of one who has been buffeted by fate and is no longer certain of his values. This poem, then, is more typical of Kavanagh's post-trial mood than "Inscription for the Tomb of the Unknown Warrior." When he was physically broken and emotionally unsettled, his initial analysis of the self proved disconcerting.

By the summer of 1955 Kavanagh's mood began to change. The financial aid and the emotional comfort he received from such friends as John Ryan, John Jordan, Senator Owen Ryan, and Archbishop John Charles McQuaid, among others, eased his recovery and, with his health nearly restored, he began to view his position more optimistically. By 1956 he was well into his rebirth, as he liked to call it, and the depression and discomforts of the libel action and his illness were behind him. In his final lecture at University College Dublin he remarked that his analysis of the self had taught him that loneliness was not a personal preserve but a state inhabited by many.

While his new spirit of understanding and acceptance took the form of simple lyricism in his poetry, in his prose it evidenced itself through a mellowed didacticism. In place of the raging criticism of the late 1940s and early 1950s, which concentrated on exposé and satire, the tempered philosophizing of the late 1950s and early 1960s tended to focus on positive explication. Typical instances of this new approach are the articles and essays he published in the *National Observer, Creation, X,* and *Nonplus.* In "The Poetic Spirit," for example, which appeared in the August, 1957, number of *Creation,* he speaks in a subdued manner about many of the subjects he had hotly contested for years in *The Standard, Envoy,* and *Kavanagh's Weekly.* Though the article is tinged by self-justification and was no doubt intended partly as a defense of his literary powers and a statement of his return to the critical arena, it demonstrates the positive approach to literature that he adopted soon after his spiritual rebirth. Familiar platitudes about the poet's nature are mixed with warnings against the dangers of mediocrity and praise for Parnassian glory; yet the basic intention is celebration rather than condemnation. The strong dogmaticism of his previous forays against the philistines is replaced by a spirit of reflection and affirmation.

Though Kavanagh abandoned the mask of the crusading journalist, the new pose he had adopted by the early 1960s, that of the pastoral prophet, occasionally slipped and revealed the old anger. Because of this, the image of the poet reborn that he wished to present did not always fit the image he affected in some of his public statements. For a time it was as if there were two Kavanaghs existing simultaneously. The private, poetic Kavanagh was detached, concerned with the celebration of self and the personal values that made life good, while the public lecturer often engaged in the rather repetitious arguments against the dead and the dull. Still, it was only in rare instances that he demonstrated the vigor that marked his harsh criticism in *Envoy* and *Kavanagh's Weekly.* In most of the columns in the *Irish Farmers' Journal* and in such essays as "From Monaghan to the Grand Canal" and "Suffering and Literature," when he did strike out at his old enemies, charlatanism and mediocrity, it seemed as if he was repeating former harangues not so much because he believed what he was saying was true, or even necessary, but because he felt it was expected of him. He admitted as much when he remarked in the course of a lecture that "When I take up my position here I am abandoning a private reality for a public illusion."[3] Perhaps his occasional lapses into invective can best be explained by his desire to exploit his former image for financial gain.

III *Phoenix on the Grand Canal*

The poetry Kavanagh wrote after 1954 clearly depicts his changing mood and his sense of spirtual rebirth. The most important poems of this period are "Prelude," "Canal Bank Walk," and "Lines Written on a Seat on the Grand Canal, Dublin, 'Erected to the Memory of Mrs. Dermot O'Brien.'" These poems suggest the range of his subjects and themes and mark the course of his creative growth. "Prelude," which was written shortly before the rebirth, illustrates quite clearly Kavanagh's concern with maintaining the appearance of a confident and successful poet. As its title suggests, the poem is a prelude of things to come. Kavanagh's characterization of himself as

> . . . one
> Who knows that art's a kind of fun;
> That all true poems laugh inwardly
> Out of grief-born intensity.

foreshadows the image of the poet that will emerge from "Canal Bank Walk," "The Hospital," and other poems of the late 1950s. Many of the subjects on which his poetic vision will focus are suggested in "Prelude." He notes in the third stanza, for example, that it is to nature rather than to society that the poet must turn if he wishes to realize the fulfillment of his talent. From this premise he concludes that

> . . . satire is unfruitful prayer
> Only wild shoots of pity there,
> And you must go inland and be

> Lost in compassion's ecstasy,
> Where suffering soars in summer air—
> The millstone has become a star.

The "inland" to which the poet must turn is his own soul. By objectively observing the self, he can transform personal pain into meaningful experience by his poetic imagination. It is coming to see the self as an example of life lived intensely that makes any emotional experience potentially valuable as subject matter for literature. According to Kavanagh's thinking at this time, "If a work remains tragic then it has not been detached from the author's personal life."[4]

"Prelude" concludes in a spirit of affirmation and hope. The simple listing of familiar details, the love act Kavanagh terms it in "The Hospital," creates a bond between the poet and his surroundings:

> Gather the bits of road that were
> Not gravel to the traveller
> But eternal lanes of joy
> On which no man who walks can die.
> Bring in the particular trees
> That caught you in their mysteries,
> And love again the weeds that grew
> Somewhere specially for you.
> Collect the river and the stream
> That flashed upon a pensive theme,
> And a positive world make,
> A world man's world cannot shake.

This synecdochical assembling of detail celebrates the past and foreshadows the future pastoral spirit of Kavanagh's rebirth. It is the reorientation of the self into nature that will restore Kavanagh's spiritual strength. "Prelude" ends with a resolution to practice the wisdom his reawakening has brought him:

> So now my gentle tiger burning bright
> In the forest of no-yearning
> Walk on serenely, do not mind
> That Promised Land you thought to find,
> Where the worldly-wise and rich take over
> The mundane problems of the lover,
> Ignore Power's schismatic sect,
> Lovers alone lovers protect.

One of the significant effects of Kavanagh's rebirth was that he again emphasized the visible rather than the ideological in his poetry. As he had in the best of his apprenticeship poems, he concentrated on rendering verse portraits of his surroundings. A good example is "The Hospital," a sonnet depicting the world through which he moved while he was confined to the Rialto Hospital. The emphasis on the visible is clearly manifested by his deliberate use of concrete language to establish a motif of contrasts. The plain, rather ugly interior of his ward is contrasted with the simple beauty of the hospital grounds to show that the poetic imagination is stimulated by both the common and the banal.

Emphasis on the visible also contributes to the effectiveness of two of Kavanagh's other important rebirth poems, "Canal Bank Walk" and "Lines Written on a Seat on the Grand Canal, Dublin." In "Canal Bank Walk" the beauty of the canal's green water and leafy trees draws Kavanagh's attention to the subtle vitality of nature. The poem's opening lines record both the setting of his poetic baptism and the nature of his spiritual rebirth. It is principally by depicting the excitement of the habitual, the ordinary, that Kavanagh hopes to vitalize the self. He stresses this intention in the last six lines where, in a prayer-like tone, he asks for a communion of the self with nature:

> O unworn world enrapture me, enrapture me in a web
> Of fabulous grass and eternal voices by a beech,
> Feed the gaping need of my senses, give me ad lib
> To pray unselfconsciously with overflowing speech
> For this soul needs to be honoured with a new
>   dress woven
> From green and blue things and arguments that
>   cannot be proven.

"Lines Written on a Seat on the Grand Canal, Dublin" is similar to "Canal Bank Walk" in its emphasis on the visual. There is the same use of concrete language to depict the canal bank as a "Parnassian island."

> A swan goes by head low with many apologies,
> Fantastic light looks through the eyes of bridges—
> And look! a barge comes bringing from Athy
> And other far-flung towns mythologies.

However, the poem lacks the spiritual intensity of "Canal Bank Walk." Concerned with celebrating the spirit of rebirth rather than with describing the event itself, "Lines Written on a Seat on the Grand Canal, Dublin" communicates the change that has taken place in Kavanagh's view of the self. It is a picture of the poet at peace, no longer troubled by the pain of disorientation or by the enigma of failure. He has succeeded in being enraptured by his surroundings and expresses this joy in his wish to be commemorated "with no hero-courageous/Tomb—just a canal-bank seat for the passer-by."

IV A New Habitation for a New Soul

Refreshed by his symbolic baptism, Kavanagh in one of his first acts after his rebirth sought to disclaim nearly all of the creative work he had produced from 1937 to 1954. *The Green Fool* was condemned as a stage-Irish autobiography; *The Great Hunger* was dismissed as underdeveloped comedy; and *A Soul for Sale* was rejected as thin romanticism. Only *Tarry Flynn* and the early *Ploughman and Other Poems* were acknowledged as having literary value. Kavanagh had several motives for rejecting what many criticis considered to be his finest writing. He touched on most of them in an introduction he wrote in May, 1960, for the BBC broadcast of *The Great Hunger*. Remarking that *The Great Hunger* placed too much emphasis on the woes of the poor, he suggested that the poem was marred by defective vision. To prevent this the poet should look upon his material with detachment. Because the case made for the plight of the rural poor is slanted to show the agonies they were forced to endure, Kavanagh held that the poem lacked the true repose of poetry. He attempted to clarify this when he remarked that

I'm afraid I'm too involved in *The Great Hunger;* the poem remains a tragedy because it is not completely born. Tragedy is underdeveloped comedy: tragedy fully explored becomes comedy. We can see it and we are not afraid. Because of these things, I am of the opinion that *The Great Hunger* . . . is a cry, a howl, and cries and howls die in the distances.[5]

His thinking here was no doubt conditioned by the fact that *The Great Hunger,* being his most successful creative effort, symbolized his literary goals of the 1940s and his commitment to social and cultural criticism. Since he had now abandoned this commitment for his doctrine of not caring, *The Great Hunger* and all that it represented was contradictory to his revised image of the poet. Thus, by rejecting this poem and his other creative achievements of the 1940s he was really rejecting his approach to literature, his "messianic compulsion," as he termed it in his preface to *Collected Poems*, that had brought about his failure to extend his poetic powers and achieve an understanding of the self.

In a sense, Kavanagh's act of rejection was motivated as much by the desire to stress his rebirth as it was by the need to dismiss his past failures. He never missed an opportunity to mention his rebirth. In lectures, letters, essays, poems, and autobiographical sketches he told his public how the summer of 1955 found him a changed man. Because of its importance to his last creative efforts and because he came to believe so strongly in it, his rebirth cannot be passed over lightly. Despite its obvious romantic appeal to him, the idea of beginning anew, of being reborn, seems to have a basis in reality, for it did produce changes in both his thinking and his writing. At the heart of the rebirth was objective stock-taking, the ability to look at himself and all that had happened to him without self-pity. This objectivity, or detachment as Kavanagh often called it, was occasioned by the need to continue in the face of the pain caused by the libel case and his illness and enabled him to set up for himself a spiritual home where the soul would be safe from the enemies of the imagination.

In pursuing this goal, Kavanagh made a number of changes in his practice of poetry. One of his first acts was to renounce satire as a mode for verse. This accompanied the dismissal of *The Great Hunger* and *A Soul for Sale* mentioned above. Other changes involved specific adjustments of certain principles evolved during his middle period. The principle of the poet as teacher, for example, which he stressed so often in his film and book reviews and in his *Envoy* diaries, was retained and reasserted in several public statements.[6] By changing the substance of his teaching from social awareness to self-enlightenment, Kavanagh was able to retain the poet's pedagogical function without compromising his new creative ideals. He also continued to preach the power of the creative imagination. Other concerns, such as his fetish with nationalism and his belief in an artist's need for an audience, were revised to accommodate the spirit of his rebirth.

These principles were supplemented with a number of new ideas about the theory and practice of poetry—ideas born of his strong belief in the comic muse. To Kavanagh, comedy was the natural outgrowth of detachment, while tragedy was occasioned by involvement. Based upon this distinction, he concluded that for the poet who sought the true repose of poetry "There is only one Muse, the Comic Muse. In Tragedy there is always something of a lie. Great poetry is always comic in the profound sense. Comedy is abundance of life."[7]

He underscored the importance of the comic muse in "From Monaghan to the Grand Canal" when he remarked that "A work that is inspired by the comic spirit has a sense of values, of courage and rectitude." To assure these values in his writing Kavanagh sought to infuse his poetry with an enthusiasm for life. "Winter" is a typical attempt to reflect the comic spirit by celebrating enthusiasm:

> that winter arrival . . . made me
> Feel younger, less of a failure, it was actually
>   earlier
> Than many people thought; there were possibilities
> For love, for South African adventure, for fathering
>   a baby[,]
> For taking oneself in hand, catching on without a
>   scare me, or
> Taking part in a world war, joining up at the start
>   of hostilities.

In other poems, such as "If You Ever Go to Dublin Town" and "Song at Fifty," enthusiasm is an important aspect of the celebration of the self.

Another method of producing the comic spirit lay in a return to the pastoral simplicity of his apprenticeship. Though the repose of his early lyric verse was not always as detached as he liked to believe, certain poems featured a zest for life and literature that he now sought in his post - 1955 poetry. To give unity to his early and later poems Kavanagh coined the phrase "departure and return" in the late 1950s. He explained in the *Irish Farmers' Journal:*

What I have learned in all my years is that we learn in life to arrive back where we started. We learn to be simple and we learn how to make a virtue out of necessity.

Being simple is a very hard thing to achieve. It requires great courage not to be ashamed. We are inclined to put on a show. When I lived in the country . . . I wrote a poem called "Shancoduff" and according to some recent critics I never improved on it. So it appears that my long journey and all my bad times and struggles were for nothing.[8]

In *Self Portrait* he was more concise:

There are two kinds of simplicity, the simplicity of going away and the simplicity of return. The last is the ultimate in sophistication. In the final simplicity we don't care whether we appear foolish or not. We talk of things that earlier would embarrass. We are satisfied with being ourselves, however small.[9]

The final simplicity is marked by the wisdom of the journey. It is essentially this wisdom that gives the best of Kavanagh's later poems their insight. He liked to think that he had returned to his original point of departure, symbolized for him by the decision to leave the farm for Dublin. The truth of the matter is that in attempting to return he really began a new journey, because what he sought was not so much an understanding of the self as repose and detachment.

This journey can be traced through a number of his poems written between 1956 and 1958. "Come Dance with Kitty Stobling," "Song at Fifty," "Is," and "To Hell with Commonsense" indicate the course of his travels in pursuit of the comic muse. In "Come Dance with Kitty Stobling," originally titled "High Journey" when it was first published in *Recent Poems*, the general route of the self's travels is marked out. He begins the journey by renouncing his former concern with popular success. In the opening lines,

> No, no, no, I know I was not important as I moved
> Through the colourful country, I was but a single
> Item in the picture, the namer not the beloved.

he states his renunciation and affirms his new concept of the poet. The next nine lines are given to an explanation of the image he had of himself as a creative artist. He notes that he had

> a myth that was a lie but it served:
> Trees walking across the crests of hills and
> my rhyme
> Cavorting on mile-high stilts and the unnerved
> Crowds looking up with terror in their rational
> faces.

Recalling this image of the self and denying its validity is necessary to prepare the way for a return to the comic mode, the "madness" of his earliest poetic efforts, as he terms it in the poem's last line:

> I had a very pleasant journey, thank you sincerely
> For giving me my madness back, or nearly.

"To Hell with Common Sense" is essentially a statement about the pseudo-ideals that distracted him from his quest for the comic. It reaffirms the rejection made in the opening lines of "Come Dance with Kitty Stobling" and clarifies what he believed caused his creative failure in the 1940s. Stating that "More kicks than pense/We get from commonsense," Kavanagh goes on to detail the nature of his previous failure. He points out that common sense, which in the context of the poem includes critical sense, blocks out the inspiration of the comic muse. Common sense in poetry is a sign of that sort of involvement that produces didactic rather than detached poems. Since he had, in the spirit of his rebirth, rejected this approach, he concludes:

> Therefore I say to hell
> With all reasonable
> Poems in particular
> We want no secular
> Wisdom plodded together
> By concerned fools.

Only recently a fool himself, according to his new criteria, he speaks from experience when he belittles those poets who devote themselves to writing well-reasoned verses:

> Let them wear out nerve and bone
> Those who would have it that way
> But in the end nothing that they
> Have achieved will be in the shake up
> In the final Wake Up.

He concludes his rejection of the common-sense approach to poetry by announcing his discovery "That through the hole in reason's ceiling/We can fly to knowledge/Without ever going to college."

Kavanagh made other discoveries in his quest of the comic muse.

In "Song at Fifty" he acknowledges his surprise "To find experience/Where I feared that I/Had no such currency." "The Wonders of Love" announces his discovery that "It takes half a lifetime to learn/To be abandoned, to yearn/For no respectable fame." However, the most important discovery is contained in "Is"; the discovery that lies at the end of the journey and signals the return to detachment. Realizing that "The important thing is not/To imagine one ought/Have something to say,/A *raison d'être*, a plot for the play[,]" Kavanagh exclaims:

> The only true teaching
> Subsists in watching
> Things moving or just colour
> Without comment from the scholar.
> To look on is enough
> In the business of love.

This is the repose born of not caring. The poet exercises his talent by recording and celebrating what excites his creative imagination. He refrains from commenting on the vision his poems project because it is unnecessary and it hinders the reader's perception. Put simply, the poet's function is to

> Name for the future
> The everydays of nature
> And without being analytic
> Create a great epic[.]

This was the main lesson that Kavanagh learned from his assessment of himself and his poetry and it became the ideal he praised throughout the period of creative growth that followed his rebirth.

Ironically, Kavanagh preached this ideal more vigorously than he practiced it and frequently violated its basic tenets against didacticism. Many of the poems and most of the prose he wrote after 1957 contain references to and lessons about the poet's function. Terms such as *gaiety, detachment, repose,* and *comic* became familiar jargon in nearly all of his statements about poets and poetry. Had he lectured less about his new ideals, had he left his poetry to speak for itself, perhaps such commentators as Douglas Sealy and John Montague would have had higher praise for the poems Kavanagh wrote after his rebirth. The responses of these

critics are typical of the remarks made by those who surveyed
Kavanagh's poetry and found his last creative efforts less impressive
than the poems of his earlier periods.[10] While some of the critical
charges leveled against the work Kavanagh produced after 1955 are
unsupportable, particularly the charge that his last poems are all
merely occasional verse, the criticism that he talks more about comedy and repose than renders it seems justified. Indeed, when he rejected *The Great Hunger* because of its emphasis on the analytical,
and when he dismissed the whole of *A Soul for Sale*, including those
poems in which he honestly probed and analyzed the self, he denied
one of the most important functions of the poet. Kavanagh wrote
some fine poems after 1955; however, his failure to "create a great
epic/Without being analytic" was due to the limitations of his revised definition of the poet. Fortunately, he often broke his new rules
in pursuing the same sort of self-analysis found in the better parts of
A Soul for Sale.

V   *God and Man*

In addition to self-analysis, Kavanagh's post-rebirth poetry
probes the relationship between God and man. This is not surprising when it is remembered that throughout his creative career
Kavanagh believed poetry to be essentially a religious experience.
To him the poet was a theologian who, through the medium of
creativity, attempted to explain man's spiritual position by interpreting the revelation contained in nature. It was no doubt this concern with the religious quality of poetry that led him to the bap-
tismal metaphor he adopted to explain the resurgence of his poetic
powers after his trial and illness. Baptism, rebirth, and redemption,
all acknowledged and celebrated in various pieces from "Canal
Bank Walk" to *Self Portrait*, served as unifying symbols to link the
renewed spiritual vitality and poetic vision of his last years to the
Christian motifs that underlie most of his apprenticeship poems. At
no time did Kavanagh ever abandon his Christian vision of life.

In Kavanagh's mind Christian meant Catholic. On more than one
occasion he stressed his belief that there was a defect in Protestant-
ism, a passion for self-interest, which reduced Protestants to
knavery and foolishness, particularly when they ventured into art.[11]
Because of this, they failed to take the broad, objective view that in
Kavanagh's opinion characterized Christianity. As to his own Christian position, he once wrote that "I am a Catholic though not of the

Lourdes-Fatima variety. And. . .I believe that, accepted pragmatically, Catholicism is the perfect measuring rule for every human endeavor."[12] A specific aspect of Catholicism that appealed to Kavanagh in his last years was monasticism. Reflecting over his stay in the Rialto Hospital in one of his weekly *Irish Farmers' Journal* pieces, he commented that the pleasure he derived from his stay in the hospital was partly due to the joy that comes from embracing the monastic life. He expressed this theme in "The Hospital," implying that acceptance and joy spring from perceiving the beauty of simple things. It is the excitement of snatching "out of time the passionate transitory," made possible by the soul's submission to the natural order of its surroundings and the abandonment of worldly values, that vitalizes one's spirit.

This theme runs through the series of poems entitled, "Three Coloured Sonnets." The act of viewing and the process of contemplating the "passionate transitory" are expressed differently in each of the sonnets. In "The One," God's presence in nature is revealed by the array of colors in humble scenes and backward places "Where no one important ever looked." This perception, fleeting as the bloom of spring flowers, lifts the poet's sprit and he is able to view, through the beauty of the scene, God's greatness, "the One and the Endless, the Mind that baulked/The profoundest of mortals." "Miss Universe," unlike "The One," presents a clearer vision of God:

> I learned something of the nature of God's mind,
> Not the abstract Creator but He who caresses
> The daily and nightly earth; He who refuses
> To take failure for an answer till again and
>   again is worn.

Here the vision is more specific and the poet's imagination is capable of translating the perception and, snatching it out of time, recording it in a poem. In the final sonnet, "Yellow Vestment," the insight springs from a private symbol rather than from self-assessment as it does in "Miss Universe." The "yellow vestment" is a "power-invoking habit" that enables the man who wears it to see life without hate or resentment and to elevate himself above base concerns. These three sonnets, like his other poems about God, communicate the spirituality that was revived by Kavanagh's rebirth.

VI   *Technical Adjustments*

To express the various themes and ideas that he pursued in his post-1955 poetry, Kavanagh altered both his approach and his technique. He wrote to his brother Peter in July, 1959, that he was "writing verse in a new style," and later, in October of the same year, that he "was writing a new kind of poem with new words."[13] In his desire to stress celebration rather than analysis, Kavanagh concluded that "Real technique is a spiritual quality, a condition of the mind, or an ability to invoke a particular condition of the mind. Lack of technique gives us shallowness . . . Technique is a method of being sincere. Technique is a method of getting at life."[14] More specifically, he explained in one of his extramural lectures that

the business of technique [is] to provide us with a means to reveal ourselves truthfully without being silly, mawkish, or in any way to speak that would make us unhappy. The purpose of technique is to enable us to detach our experience from ourselves and see it as a thing apart.[15]

To develop new techniques to express his themes and to communicate the comic spirit, Kavanagh experimented with various elements of versification, particularly form and rhyme. The form he used to greatest advantage was the sonnet. For a period of three years, from 1956 through 1959, nearly all of the poems that he wrote were sonnets or variations of the sonnet. He was attracted to this form because it was traditionally associated with love poetry and he had now made love one of his major themes. The sonnet also appealed to him because, as he once remarked, "its strict rules . . . force the mind to moral activity but is not itself forced."[16]

Rhyme, perhaps more than any other element of versification, seems to have attracted Kavanagh's attention after 1955. He noted his special interst in rhyme in a brief note he wrote to introduce "Important Statement"[17] in an American anthology entitled, *Poet's Choice:*

Over the past few years—since about 1956—I have learned the magical, imagination-stimulating quality of outrageous rhyming: clichés, species, Nietzsche's.[18]

One of the main values of rhyme used in this manner was its subtle emphasis of the comic that Kavanagh preached so often during these years. Justifying his experiments with rhyme, he wrote in "From Monaghan to the Grand Canal":

I discovered that the important thing above all was to avoid taking oneself sickly seriously. One of the good ways of getting out of this respectability is the judicious use of slang and of outrageous rhyming. [19]

In addition to "Important Statement," such poems as "A Summer Morning Walk," "The Gambler: a Ballet with Words," and "Mermaid Tavern" provide good examples of Kavanagh's outrageous rhyming. However, one of the best examples is "Puzzle." Here he combines his free use of the sonnet with slang, full rhyme, and slant rhyme to declare:

> The rhyme's the thing, I assure you I stake
> My reputation on this most plain assertion
> And those who know me know I'm not the person
> To back a horse that can't accelerate.

His previous track record aside, it seems in this particular case Kavanagh well may have bet on the wrong horse. The judiciousness of his rhymes has been criticized by a number of writers, particularly Hayden Carruth and Douglas Sealy. [20] Even such friends as John Jordan and John Ryan concede that Kavanagh's rhymes often distract from the effectiveness of certain poems.

Kavanagh's problems with versification spring from several sources. The lifelong need to draw attention to himself and to his writing was no doubt a factor in his choice of language. A survey of his earlier poetry indicates that even before his rebirth he experimented with slang, slant-rhyme, and doggerel verse. The satires of the late 1940s provide ample evidence of this. Also, while some of his careless rhyming might be explained by a desire to underscore his informality, to argue that Kavanagh purposely wrote awkward poetry, or that he intentionally marred certain poems to stress his belief in detachment, is dubious at best. The truth of the matter lies in the simple fact that his creative power was no longer what it had been. The lapses in his poetry are due more to a failure of ability than to any design to shock his readers or draw attention to himself. The proof of this is clearly evident in the last dozen or so poems that he wrote.

VII   *Last Poems: a Return to Inniskeen*

Generally, these last poems are concerned with country life, creative assessment, and spiritual resolution. There are two groups of country poems: the first written from 1959 to 1961, the second from 1964 to 1966. The first group, occasioned by his return to Inniskeen for health and financial reasons, features a curious mixture of agony and affirmation. His poetic response to this stay in Inniskeen was similar to the moods and the themes expressed in many of his apprenticeship poems. For example, the sense of isolation that underlies "Shancoduff" and "To a Blackbird" is present in a number of these later poems. Also evident is a concern with seeing the self clearly against the complexities of rural life. In "Having to Live in the Country" rural existence is portrayed as a private hell for the sensitive man:

> in wild, wet Monaghan
> Exiled from thought and feeling,
> A mean brutality reigns:
> It is really a horrible position to be in
> And I equate myself with Dante
> And all who have to live outside civilization.
> It isn't a question of place but of people[.]

"Living in the Country: I" contains the same reference to exile, but the poet's mood is more optimistic. Echoing the statement of the self in "To a Blackbird," Kavanagh comments that

> In many ways it is a good thing to be cast
>   into exile
> Among strangers
> Who have no inkling
> Of The Other Man concealed
> Monstrously musing in a field.
> For me they say a Rosary
> With many a glossary.

The nature of rural exile is examined at some length in both "Living in the Country: I" and "Living in the Country: II." The opening lines of "Living in the Country: I" create a mood of optimism and nostalgia:

> It was the Warm Summer, that landmark
> In a child's mind, an infinite day
> Sunlight and burnt grass
> Green grasshoppers on the railway slopes
> The humming of the wild bees
> The whole summer during the school holidays
> Till the blackberries appeared.
> Yes, a tremendous time that summer stands
> Beyond the grey finites of normal weather.

The lyricism of these lines is reminiscent of Kavanagh's best apprentice writing. Having established this reflective tone, he goes on to explain his reaction to life among "small farmers in the North of Ireland." Their stubbornness, their fear of intellectual life, and their distrust of city manners are no longer as offensive to him as they were before his training "in the slum pubs of Dublin/Among the most offensive class of all—/The artisans." Since he was conditioned by the years of battling the philistines, the attitudes of his country neighbors merely confirmed his original hypothesis that the poet must seek through his work a spiritual habitation outside the bounds of his practical existence. The poet's world is a world of love, and it is sustained by a detachment and a celebration of the self as it exists in loving watery hills or the banks of a canal. The comfort, then, of living in the country results from the pleasure the poet takes in being stimulated by his surroundings. While he is exiled among the people, he is at home in the fields and on the roads.

"Living in the Country: II," written four years after "Living in the Country: I," continues to celebrate the joy of living close to the source of revelation and to the beauty of nature:

> In the disused railway siding
> (O railway that came up from Enniskillen)
> A new living is spreading
> Dandelions that grow from wagon-grease
> I stand on the platform
> And peace, perfect peace
> Descends on me.

Unlike "Living in the Country: I," however, there is an element of disorder in the poet's world. He is disturbed by a sense of personal loss, by a failure to sustain the inner balance that enabled him to live apart from the blind, artless neighbors of his youth and the

philistines and artisans of his middle years. Part of the poem is
given over to an assessment of his present condition. He notes with
some pain that he has been a bore and that he has idled away his
time roaring and cursing at his misfortunes. There are references to
his lack of money, his forced retreat to Inniskeen, his need of an
apartment and friends. But these are merely peripheral difficulties.
The real problem is centered in the self, in an awareness of the
blurring of his artistic vision and the ebbing of his creative energy
to articulate his ideas. The poem itself is a clear demonstration of
the gravity of his poetic failings. A rough and uneven mixture of
doggerel and lyric verse, of half-rhymes and forced rhymes, of
awkward syntax, and of satire and protest, the poem foreshadows
Kavanagh's literary collapse and shows him adrift on the wreckage
of his sinking talent. Despite all of this, "Living in the Country: II"
has a veneer of optimism. Perhaps unaware of the seriousness of the
problem, or perhaps clinging to the hope that his creative energies
will return, Kavanagh attempts to portray himself as a man in full
control of his destiny. He declares that

> I never suffer from malnu-
> Trition. Or need for grog
> I make a product I can easily flog
> I am a small country exporting
> The pill of meaning to those
> Whom the condition is hurting
> At this moment I can make spells
> Whatever I say goes
> Come London-Irish to me your voided souls
> Shall not be left unfilled
> I am more than a pub or club
> I am the madhouse that spilled,
> Spills, the true reason
>   . . .
>   I am self-centered
> But bunch of bums
> I throw you these bewitching crumbs
> I give you the womb
> Of the poem.

But this is merely the boast of a man haunted by inner fears who
is shouting to give himself courage. A more significant statement
comes earlier in the poem when, reflecting over his return to Inniskeen, he muses:

> When first walking along these roads
> Nobody but myself walked there
> But wait a minute, an hour a day
> There are men and women behaving
> There are girls in troubled love
> And all that I need to do is weave the action
> And many may do things quite valuable.
>
> . . .
>
> I know what I must write if I can
> This is the beginning of my Five Year Plan
> Concerned am I with the activities of my own man.

This is an expression of genuine hope. By weaving the action, by writing objectively and with detachment, he may be able to regain his poetic equilibrium and his creative vitality.

The other country poems that Kavanagh wrote during his first extended stay in Inniskeen deal with far less serious matters. Two of the most typical are "Requiem for a Mill" and "July Evening." Both poems are vivid recollections of lighter moments. "July Evening" is essentially an occasional poem which celebrates the pleasure of an evening walk. "Requiem for a Mill" was written to commemorate Moyles Mill, a local landmark which was torn down in the spring of 1958. The poem's style is similar to certain lyrics in *Ploughman and Other Poems*. Written in couplets, the poem suffers occasionally from Kavanagh's use of outrageous rhyming. However, unlike much of the poetry he wrote during the late 1950s, here he exhibits a firm control over rhythm and language.

Kavanagh's second group of country poems share with their earlier counterparts the themes of isolation and personal exile. In "My Native Village," he makes his position clear in the opening lines:

> Exiled in the village of my birth
> Where everyone is old and rude without mirth
> And I am thirty light years from the earth.

The rest of the poem is given to a catalog of the problems he encounters in trying to accommodate his rural acquaintances. He notes that some consider him a snob, while others continue to view him as a fool in love with watery hills. Throughout the poem he stresses that he was and is an outsider in his birthplace.

A more serious poem is "Autobiography Continued." This

monologue contains an interesting and fairly accurate statement of Kavanagh's addiction to alcohol at the time:

> Two months ago I was in the rats,
> Alcoholic poisoning. That's
> Nothing to laugh about. My legs
> Buckled at the knees
> My stomach groaned up its last dregs
> And I had hallucinations.
> There were people in my bedroom
> Shouting at me and I ran twisted
> Literally, to a sittingroom
> Crowded with visitors.

The poem concludes with a cry for release from his rural confinement:

> From my rural redoubt
> Most loathsome spot
> I shout and I shout
> Let me out, let me out.

The other important theme treated in these last country poems is his concern with the failure of his creative talent. By this time, when Kavanagh confronted this problem seriously, he exhibited little hope that it would or could be solved. His health was undoubtedly the most important factor. Years earlier he had noted in a letter to his brother Peter that it took great energy to write well. This was particularly true in Kavanagh's case because he was a spontaneous poet who relied upon mood and inspiration. With his health gone, he was often depressed and almost constantly in pain. While he never lost his desire to write, his creative faculties and his ability to concentrate were severely damaged by his poor physical condition. In view of this, it is not difficult to understand why the few poems that he did write during his last three years are undistinguished. One of his better efforts is "Thus a Poet Dies," which records the struggle he was having with his talent. Reflecting on his past achievements in writing verse in the country he noted that

> . . . once upon a time
> These days could inflame
> And I'd throw loving charms

> At my two stoney farms
> That I'd sell at no price.

But the truth of his situation could not be denied. Seeing this clearly himself, he acknowledged that

> I am here in my own acres again
> Looking around me, thinking
> Thoughts that have no life
> Though it is mid-summer I've
> No wish to rhapsodise,
> Thus a poet dies.

VIII   *"In Blinking Blankness"*

In the period between Kavanagh's first lengthy stay in Inniskeen in 1959 and his last sojourn there in 1965 - 66, he wrote a number of poems that clearly demonstrate the extent of his creative failure. Characterized by an almost pathetic honesty and by serious technical lapses, this work signals the end of Kavanagh's poetic development. A typical example of this uneven and often empty writing is the lengthy poem, "The Gambler: a Ballet with Words." While some of the poem's weaknesses might be explained away by the fact that it was rather hastily written to satisfy a commission Kavanagh received from the Guinness Company, its general lack of substance, its amateurish use of rhyme, and its fragmented and often nonsensical syntax are faults that even the apprentice Kavanagh would have condemned. Perhaps embarrassed by these flaws, Kavanagh prefaced the piece with a brief explanation that begins:

> Here we have a work of fiction, purporting
> To portray the ways of the poet-artist,
> It has gone wrong in places, missed
> The secret of love—the gift
> Of the poet's knowledge[.]

And in another section of the poem he openly admits:

> I have nothing to announce
> On any subject yet once
> I was full of bounce[.]

The worst of his final efforts include "About Reason, Maybe," "A Summer Morning Walk," "The Same Again," "That Garage," and "Literary Adventures." All of these were written between 1961 and 1963 and share the same facile attitude toward poetry that marks his approach in "The Gambler: a Ballet with Words." Also, each of them illustrates a lack of substance due to a loss of poetic vision. Instead of charging the varied subjects that he treats with the excitement of the creative imagination, instead of exploding the atoms of common, ordinary experience, all Kavanagh succeeds in achieving is an amplification of the banal babbling that had replaced his post-rebirth lyricism. "A Summer Morning Walk" shows the extent of his loss. In these lines:

> I meet a man whom I once had pumped
> With ideas, he was sad and humped
> Like a market that had downward slumped.
>
> The ideas I had upon him forced
> Were gone and left him much worse the worst
> And to think how amusingly he had discoursed.

a number of serious technical lapses are evident. In addition to mixing metaphors, forcing rhymes, inverting word order, and misusing alliteration, he fails to sustain the humor necessary to justify his rather monotonous use of doggerel.

Despite all of his technical faults and the failure of his poetic vision, Kavanagh continued to write. He partially explained his rationale for continuing in "A Summer Morning Walk":

> I just want to assure all
> That a poem made is a cure-all
> Of any soul-sickness. Toolooral!
>
>   . . .
>
> If I can lie on the grass, feel no remorse
> For idling, I have worked at verse
> And exorcised a winter's curse.

As in the past, he believed that he could solve his problems by writing them out of his system. To a degree he was right. He did manage, before he died, to regain some of his former energy and write a few good poems. Among the best of these are "An Insult," "Rampas Point," and "Yeats." While these poems are not free of those technical lapses common to nearly all of his last poems, they feature an honesty of expression that redeems them from whatever faults they suffer. It is a tribute to Kavanagh and a mark of the true poet that even though he was suffering both physical and creative agonies he could detach himself and view his position without self-pity. He had the strength of character to admit his weakness and to assess his failing vision with accuracy and with candor. The poems "In Blinking Blankness: Three Efforts" and "Sensational Disclosures!" are clear, if rather crude, demonstrations of this. But perhaps Kavanagh's most complete and most successful statement of his final position is "Personal Problem." Here he writes candidly that

> . . . I can only
> Tell of my problem without solving
> Anything.
>
> . . .
> So there it is my friends. What am I to do
> With the void growing more awful every hour?
> I lacked a classic discipline. I grew
> Uncultivated and now the soil turns sour[.]

After autumn of 1966 Kavanagh no longer made any serious efforts to revive his talent, and the final group of country poems that he wrote between 1964 and 1966 brought his poetic career to an end. It is fitting that his last writing was done in Inniskeen. Unfortunately, these poems are flawed by blurred vision and technical failure. Kavanagh's realization of his problem and its seriousness may account for his decision to stop writing poetry. In any case, his deteriorating health made writing of any type very difficult, though he did manage prefaces for *Collected Pruse* and *The Autobiography of William Carleton*. Whatever hopes he may have had to return to poetry ended with his final physical collapse and death in November, 1967.

CHAPTER 6

Behind the Holy Door

T O commemorate his final extramural lecture at University College Dublin in 1956 Kavanagh composed a special poem.[1] In it he included these lines:

> I thank you and I say how proud
> That I have been by fate allowed
> To stand here having the joyful chance
> To claim my inheritance
> For most have died the day before
> The opening of the holy door.

The warmth and interest with which his lectures had been received must have seemed to Kavanagh a vindication of his recent ordeals with *The Leader* and lung cancer. No doubt he believed, at least for the moment, that he was at last on the threshold of receiving the recognition he felt he deserved. Unfortunately, his hopes were premature, a fact he himself clearly realized as indicated by his "Author's Note" to *Collected Poems*.[2] As it is now some twelve years since Kavanagh died, the time seems more opportune to look behind the holy door.

I   Critical Opinion

Any serious investigation of Kavanagh's literary career should ultimately consider not only certain specific questions about his treatment of materials, his use of language, and his artistic vision, but also more general questions about his influence on and his place in modern Anglo-Irish poetry. While many essays and articles have been written about Kavanagh, few of them offer satisfactory answers to these questions. Indeed, the most distinguishing marks of these evaluations have been unevenness and inconsistency.

140

Nearly all of the commentators who have surveyed Kavanagh's career fall easily into one of several groups. There are those who were maligned by Kavanagh and who responded in kind, countering his criticism with harsh remarks of their own.[3] Some of these writers later tempered their judgments in posthumous tributes to the poet, while others remained firm in their denials of his literary ability. A second group of critics fail in their assessments because they do not trouble themselves to examine the whole of Kavanagh's literary canon.[4] Whether due to laziness or to an ignorance of critical procedure, many of the several dozen essays, articles, and sketches that have appeared since the mid-1950s go astray in part because they lack research. With the exception of Brendan Kennelly, Douglas Sealy, and Alan Warner, most commentators make no attempt to examine closely the wide range of Kavanagh's writing and often content themselves with whatever is at hand. Because his publishing history is rather like a maze, and because important items are hidden in magazines and journals that have ceased publication, many critics frequently draw conclusions from either inaccurate or insufficient information. Academics who make use of *Collected Poems* and *Collected Pruse* do not avoid this problem because both of these books contain editorial lapses and textual errors, due no doubt to the publisher's intention to produce popular rather than scholarly collections. Other critics rely solely on *A Soul for Sale* and *Come Dance with Kitty Stobling*, ignoring Kavanagh's prose. The danger here is obvious when one remembers the close relationship between Kavanagh's poetry and his criticism. To evaluate the one without considering the other and attempt to assess with some accuracy the degree of Kavanagh's accomplishment is nearly impossible. Other groups include those who seek to praise his work by recalling their association with him; those who claim to judge the poetry when they are really judging the man; and those who abandon all objectivity in justifying his creative and technical failures because they like a portion of his work.[5]

Despite the confusion, the inaccuracies, and the twisted thinking, a number of the more balanced pieces attempt to answer basic questions about his poetry. In regard to subject matter, it is generally agreed that Kavanagh wrote perceptively about his surroundings, whether in Inniskeen or in Dublin, though there is argument over which material he handled better. The consensus of opinion seems to be that his pastoral portraits are more successful than his urban satires. Even the best of his post-1955 poems, for example, feature a return to the simplicity of his early rural lyrics. The poems about his rebirth on the banks of the Grand Canal depict the natural beauty of the scene, that bit of countryside isolated in the city that generates a new spiritual vitality. Though Kavanagh's satires should not and cannot be dismissed as lacking literary merit, it is difficult to deny that he achieved his finest poetic statements when he reflected on his country experiences and his relationship with nature.

Another issue that critics have debated is Kavanagh's use of language. Some commentators believe that the main defect in his writing is an inadequate grasp of the potentialities of language as a penetrative instrument, while others think that his power over words is a near-perfect equivalence of thought and expression. The truth lies somewhere between these two opinions. The rather monotonous and plodding language of a large number of Kavanagh's poems is not defensible. Aside from *The Great Hunger*, when he ventured into didactic poetry during the 1940s, his use of language became clumsy and, in certain poems, almost amateurish. "Adventures in the Bohemian Jungle" is a typical example. Here the bite one expects from satire is absent due, in large part, to a mis-use of language. While such poems as "Prelude" and "Father Mat" from *A Soul for Sale* demonstrate that he could employ language as a tool to strike through the surface of experience to yield up its full meaning, they are exceptions rather than the rule. Perhaps his finest and most sustained use of language during his middle period occurs in *Tarry Flynn*. Certain passages of this novel rival the best of his early and later poetry for evocative description.

There are several reasons why Kavanagh's handling of language was not consistent. The fine balance between concentration and ex-ecution that marks his best writing was disturbed whenever he shifted into the didactic voice. His critical passion appears to have been too strong for him to maintain control over language when he struck out at ideals and philosophies that offended him. Also, he often was simply careless in regard to word choice. He rarely bothered with the kind of painstaking revision that characterized Yeats's approach to the craft of poetry and, as a result, many good poems are flawed by lapses and weaknesses in diction that might have been eliminated with a little attention. However, even though he frequently broke many of the more formal conventions of rhyme and meter and often employed conversational elements in his writing, Kavanagh was sensitive to the power of language and succeeded in charging the best of his poems with an intensity of feeling that clarified his response to specific experience. Such poems as "Prelude," "The Hospital," and "Canal Bank Walk" offer ample proof of this.

The question of Kavanagh's poetic vision has caused more confusion perhaps than any other aspect of his writing. The tendency for most commentators is either to dismiss him as an uncompromising egotist or to celebrate him as a detached realist. Again, his poetry and criticism can be made to support both of these views to a degree. His *Envoy* diaries and his editorial comments in *Kavanagh's Weekly* frequently portray his failure to retain a modicum of objectivity in projecting his vision of life and literature. Too often he gives in to the temptation to preach Kavanaghisms.[6] However, he did write realistically about specific aspects of his life, providing insight into even the most commonplace experiences. Yet Kavanagh was no realist in the strict sense of the word. At times his vision is closer to naturalism than it is to realism. In "Father Mat" and *The Great Hunger*, for example, he does not portray rural life simply as it is, but as it must be, with an almost deterministic tone.

Kavanagh himself held that reality is only valuable to the poet when it is transmuted. And, while much of his poetry is based on reality, his vision of that reality is often very personal. Throughout *Ploughman and Other Poems* and particularly in *Come Dance with Kitty Stobling* he strove to portray life as he saw it from his personal point of view. In both books he transmutes his subject matter into a spiritual order one might call the reality of the soul. The same process occurs in *Tarry Flynn*. Kavanagh remarked in a letter to his brother Peter:

Here am I myself writing this novel. Can I go on telling what the people did in a peasant community? Will it have any purpose or meaning? . . . The thing is useless unless it is caught up and shown as something eternal. The power of the poet's faith [is] to synthesize.[7]

His success in *Tarry Flynn*, as in the best of his poetry, illustrates his ability to project his personal vision clearly and simply.

Kavanagh's point of view evolved primarily from his response to life, which was emotional rather than intellectual. The spontaneity that charges such poems as "To a Blackbird," "Ploughman" "The Self-Slaved," and "Come Dance with Kitty Stobling" is one sign of this. Another is the high passion that lies behind his satires and criticism. Even the tone of *The Great Hunger* is due to an emotional rather than to an intellectual reaction to life on the land. This is not to suggest that Kavanagh's mind was not focused on the subjects and themes he treats, but rather that his poetic insight operated intuitively. In place of the logic that directs the creative vision of poets like T. S. Eliot and W. B. Yeats, Kavanagh's creative faculties rely on inspiration and intuition. Artistically, he reacts rather than acts. Unlike many modern poets, his poems are not assembled piecemeal like contemporary sculptures but are delivered whole from the creative womb.

II *Self-Evaluation*

Though critics continue to argue about Kavanagh's vision and his use of language, they agree that he is one of Ireland's foremost poets. Indeed, some have hailed him as the best Irish poet since W. B. Yeats, while others have gone so far as to declare him among the finest poets in the English-speaking world. Not surprisingly, Kavanagh himself has contributed to the literature assessing his achievement and place in modern poetry. In the late 1940s and early 1950s his financial problems combined with his sense of isolation and failure and occasioned a series of interesting self-portraits. Frequently these pieces ring with self-justification. A typical example is the sketch, "The Year 2021 A.D.," which first appeared in *Envoy*. Sensitive to the criticism provoked by his monthly diary, he fantasizes that future literary historians will see him as

a man of gentle disposition, a kindly critic who lent a helping hand to every humble practitioner in the craft of writing. The myth that he was a proud, lecherous, cranky person has long since been torn to shreds. . . . His poverty did not make him thwarted or bitter as it sometimes does. He never lost his sense of humor, felt no disappointment, couldn't care less. He was a great philosopher. The secret of his success was women's affection for him. He was extremely lazy and might have made a great deal of money if he had not been so. . . . He was, it is true, capable of being crooked and secretive, but the one thing he was not was ungenerous. He hated mediocrity because it injured the good and noble.[8]

Though there may be a temptation to dismiss statements such as this as nothing more than lighthearted self-satire, beneath the humor there is an undeniable element of seriousness—and truth. He did hate mediocrity, he was neither bitter nor thwarted by poverty, and he surely suffered from laziness. One element common to other self-portraits is confidence. Despite his financial and creative difficulties, he never lost faith in his talent. At one low point in 1947 he wrote to Peter: "I feel I have the permanent stuff in myself and only need to be stirred."[9]

Toward the end of his life, however, Kavanagh did question the effectiveness of his writing. He remarked in one of his extramural lectures at University College Dublin: "I feel the utmost compassion but a compassion tinged with regret, and sometimes with annoyance, that my work is failing to produce the results I hoped for. For though but dimly perceived perhaps, I have a point of view which I have been arguing."[10] Shortly before he died this concern was voiced with more finality in an interview which appeared in *Hibernia*, the Irish fortnightly. To the query, "What do you consider is your best work," Kavanagh responded:

I don't like anything of my own. I don't like anything, I am always hoping to do something that would be good. Always believing that there were a few small items here and there which I thought were good but it's a long time ago since I thought anything of my own was any good. When you begin, I believe, you think every thing you do is almost certain of living, but as you get older, you less and less believe in your own self.[11]

Granting that Kavanagh may have exaggerated some of his remarks (he commented at the end of the interview, for example, that "a man doesn't say what he really feels through answering questions. . . We tend to speak on the surface, expressing the surface irritations of the moment."), his statements here are an indication of the dissatisfaction he felt for his writing.

Though one should not take too seriously Kavanagh's repudiation of a lifetime's work, for very often the poet is too close to his poetry to render an objective judgment, his assessment accurately reflects his poetic temperament. Throughout his last years, in interviews, prefaces, and other public statements, he protested often and loudly that his worst poems were anthologized while his best writing was neglected by critics, particularly outside Ireland. Remembering his penchant for notoriety, one cannot help feeling that many of Kavanagh's complaints about his writing were issued to draw attention to it. In many ways the problems that confronted him in his pursuit of poetry were occasioned more often by his state of mind than by his lack of education or by his rural background. It would not be incorrect to say that one of his more serious handicaps in becoming a successful poet was his personality. At the same time, however, it is his personality that vitalizes his best writing. Had he been able to direct his responses to life and literature in a more orderly and logical fashion he might have produced a more even body of work, but one lacking the intensity and clarity of vision that characterizes his better poems.

III   Legacy

Of all that has been written about him, very little has been said about his influence on other Irish writers, save a few vague remarks about a Kavanagh school of writing. It may be too early to tell the degree and the value of his influence because the poetry that will demonstrate his full impact has yet to be written. Then, too, many of the younger Irish poets who claim association with him are not read widely enough to draw serious critical attention. Still, Kavanagh was and continues to be a force in Anglo-Irish literature that is impossible to ignore. His ideas about all forms of literature have provoked considerable comment and discussion among a large number of Irish literati. Though many writers, particularly those who have suffered the ill fate of being skewered on his critical lance, consider him an outrageous if not an incoherent critic, very few dismiss his poetry. It is ironic that Kavanagh's most didactic prose, which he composed with great energy and passion, and which is accessible only to those willing to thumb through defunct periodicals and old newspapers, has been less important as an influence than the poetry he vehemently rejected late in his life. When he remarked in the course of his libel action against *The Leader* that "There will be good writers in this country, and it will be due to my work," he was, no doubt, thinking about his *Envoy* "Diary" and his editorials in *Kavanagh's Weekly*, and not about his rural lyrics and his portraits of country life.[12]

Not surprisingly of all the poems he wrote the one that has received the highest praise and that will ensure his reputation as a man of great talent is also the one that has been the most influential. Despite his remarks to the contrary, Kavanagh sensed the importance of *The Great Hunger* before he died. In a letter to his brother Peter in which he complained about the critics' lack of enthusiasm for his work, he called himself a "literary diamond mine which has been till now viciously ignored by American 'critics' and neglected by English ones," and predicted that "within a few months or a

year the critics are about to awaken to realize the enormous influence I have had on such poets as, for instance, R. S. Thomas.''[13]
Though the great awakening that he predicted has yet to occur, he
was not at all wrong about the influence of his poetry on younger
writers. His choice of R. S. Thomas as evidence of his influence was
not only quite apt, but was also an indication of the impact he
believed *The Great Hunger* had made on other poets. Even the
most casual reading of Thomas's long poem *The Minister* (1953) indicates the debt it owes to *The Great Hunger*.

The Great Hunger's influence is even more apparent in the work
being produced by some of Ireland's better younger writers. Instead
of merely imitating Kavanagh, these poets work the poetic ground
broken by *The Great Hunger*. To them, the importance of
Kavanagh's poem lies in the fact that it has opened the way and
provided a model for writing about universal themes without losing
the texture of the Irish scene. Examples of this are Richard
Murphy's *Sailing to an Island* and John Montague's *Poisoned
Lands*. While these poets treat different materials, and while they
employ form and language in different ways, they are representative of those younger writers who follow Kavanagh's practice of
treating human problems in an Irish setting without reverting to the
trite divisions of squire and peasant. One of the ironies of
Kavanagh's life is that in not being overly concerned with literary
traditions he should be praised for starting one.

However one chooses to view Kavanagh, the vitality that he
brought to Irish poetry, the lyrically articulated vision of the self
that emerges from his writing, and the final affirmation of life and
its possibilities combine to ensure his continued reputation as one of
Ireland's great literary artists.

Notes and References

Chapter One

1. The Dolmen Press, 1964, p. 12.
2. "A Memory," April 6, 1929; "A Pure White Scroll," January 19, 1929; "The Faery Land of Song," September 29, 1928; "In October," November 10, 1928; "The Pessimist," September 22, 1928; "Summer," September 15, 1928; "Thralldom," January 5, 1929; "Till Love Came," December 29, 1929; "To a Child I Know," October 13, 1928; "To a Distant Friend," June 8, 1929; "To All Children," March 23, 1929; "To a Lonely One," October 6, 1928; "To Fame," March 2, 1929; "The Tramp Woman," February 16, 1929.
3. See pp. 292 - 306.
4. During the period 1936 - 37 Kavanagh received encouraging notes from the publishing firms of Macmillan and Constable. It was principally through the aid of Helen Waddell, the English novelist, that Kavanagh made the journey from Inniskeen to London. While in London he received both financial aid and critical advice from the poet John Gawsworth, who expressed considerable interest in publishing a selection of Kavanagh's poems in his *Richard's Booklets*.
5. Rumors circulating in Dublin at the time suggested that what Gogarty really objected to was the suggestion that he had only one mistress!
6. See "Young Poet Who May Become the Irish Robert Burns," *The Daily Telegraph and Morning Post*, May 27, 1938, p. 10.
7. *Self Portrait*, p. 8.
8. P. 11.
9. See Alan Warner, *Clay Is the Word*, The Dolmen Press (Dublin, 1973), pp. 132 - 34.
10. *Horizon*, V (January 25, 1942), p. 36.
11. *Lapped Furrows*, Peter Kavanagh Hand Press (New York, 1969), pp. 148 - 49.
12. *Ibid.*, p. 171.
13. Two names frequently mentioned as authors of the "Profile" are Brendan Behan, the dramatist, and Valentine Iremonger, a minor poet of the day.
14. Rumors at the time suggested that Kavanagh filed suit principally because he wanted to win a sizable judgment and improve a rather strained financial position.
15. *Lapped Furrows*, p. 174.

16. *Collected Poems* contains most (but certainly not all) of the poetry that Kavanagh published between 1929 and 1963. That the book appeared at all is due largely to the efforts of Timothy O'Keeffe, an editor at MacGibbon & Kee with a strong interest in contemporary Irish writers. O'Keeffe was aided in his task by the poet John Montague, who selected the early poems, and by fellow editor Martin Green, who chose the later poems and is credited by Kavanagh with editing the text. Green's purpose was to provide a popular edition of Kavanagh's poems. This, plus Kavanagh's lack of interest in the collection, may account for the inconsistencies in the book's organization and text.

17. Kavanagh had very little to do with the publication of *Collected Pruse* (1967), an incomplete collection of essays, articles, exerpts from *The Green Fool* and *Tarry Flynn*, and an extensive extract from the *Irish Times'* account of Kavanagh's libel action against *The Leader*. Because of poor health, Kavanagh asked Niall Sheridan to edit the book. Sheridan assembled the text, but it was Kavanagh himself who chose to call it "Collected Pruse" rather than the more conventional "Collected Prose." According to the editorial department at MacGibbon & Kee, Kavanagh thought "prose" sounded too portentous and wished to add a touch of flippancy to the title. When he saw the book upon its publication, Kavanagh was disappointed with it and wrote: "it isn't a good collection as I didn't do it myself" (*Lapped Furrows*, p. 277).

Chapter Two

1. *The Green Fool*, p. 266.

2. Ibid., p. 271.

3. See *Self Portrait* (Dublin, 1964), pp. 9 - 10.

4. Later in his life, Kavanagh appears to have realized the effect the briefness of his education had upon him, for he wrote in *Kavanagh's Weekly* (June 7, 1952) that if you send a child to school "it is grossly unfair that through lack of money he—if he has the aptitude for it—cannot have the opportunity of going further. . . because an educated man or woman is one who knows how to measure up people, things and events, and, above all, himself—without anger, arrogance or fear" (p. 5).

5. Several of these early lyrics are included in *Lapped Furrows*. See pp. 6 - 7 for "The Band," p. 6 for "Farrelly Climbed in the Window," and p. 7 for "The Shoemaker."

6. A typical example is the theme of finding value in performing common, ordinary tasks well. Treated briefly in "The Shoemaker," this theme is one of the principal statements of *Ploughman and Other Poems*.

7. "Round the Cinemas," *The Standard*, February 22, 1946, p. 5.

8. For a list of these poems see Note 2, Chapter 1.

9. See p. 323.

10. See *Lapped Furrows*, p. 115.

11. See Ezra Pound, "A Retrospect," in *Modern Poetry: Essays in Criticism*, ed. John Hollander (New York, 1968), pp. 3 - 14.

12. *Lapped Furrows*, p. 111.

13. *The Green Fool*, pp. 263 - 64.

14. Ibid., p. 317.

15. Ibid., p. 263. *Italics mine.

16. P. 161.

17. *Lapped Furrows*, p. 27.

18. Ibid.

19. Ibid., p. 30.

20. Ibid., p. 34.

21. National Library Of Ireland Ms. 9579.

22. P. 331.

23. "Free Soul."

24. *The Green Fool*, p. 100.

25. This poem, published in the September 16, 1938, issue of *Spectator*, is not to be confused with the more famous poem of the same title which appeared in the February 15, 1930, number of the *Irish Statesman*.

26. See Padraic Fallon, "A Poet's Apprenticeship: Symbols of a Countryside," *Irish Times*, August 20, 1938, p. 7.

27. *The Green Fool*, p. 161.

28. "Re-Orientation of Irish Letters," *Irish Times*, September 21, 1935, p. 12.

Chapter Three

1. "The Wonder of Easter," *Irish Farmers' Journal*, April 1, 1961, p. 27.

2. P. 183.

Chapter Four

1. *Self Portrait*, p. 13.

2. Set in the period 1865 - 1880, "The Cobbler and the Football Team" is a romantic tale about the exploits of a young, handsome cobbler named Jack Finn. Aged twenty-five, Finn is a literary lad who, when not repairing shoes, reads widely, with a particular interest in poetry. The center of the story is the great football match between the hometown Cuchulains and the visiting club from Gatton. At a crucial moment in the match, Finn replaces the injured Cuchulain captain and then scores the winning points. The story concludes with his being proclaimed a local hero and winning the hand of the village's prettiest girl.

3. These stories include "One Summer Morning in the Month of June," *The Irish Press*, June 15, 1946; "Stars in Muddy Puddles," *The Irish Press*, April 14, 1946; "The Good Child," *The Standard*, December 24, 1947; and "The Lay of the Crooked Knight," *The Irish Press*, January 10, 1946.

4. "The Year's Best Poetry," *The Dublin Magazine*, XII (April-June, 1939), 95.

5. "Fifty Years Achievement," September 7, 1945, p. 4.

6. "Literature and the Universities," 69.

7. "Mr. Belloc Again," June 13, 1942, p. 5.

8. *Collected Pruse* (London, 1967), p. 97.

9. "A Goat Tethered Outside the Bailey," 30.

10. "Literature and the Universities," 70.

11. "A Goat Tethered Outside the Bailey," 30.

12. "Ethical Standards," *The Standard*, April 2, 1943, p. 4.

13. Ibid.

14. *Collected Pruse*, p. 25.

15. "Round the Cinemas," October 25, 1946, p. 5.

16. Ibid., February 28, 1947, p. 7.

17. "Diary," *Envoy*, II (May, 1950), 86.

18. "Colored Balloons," *The Bell*, XV (December, 1947), 18.

19. "The Gallivanting Poet," *Irish Writing*, III (November, 1947), 67.

20. "Irish Miles," *The Bell*, XIV (September, 1947), 74.

21. Ibid.

22. "Poetry in Ireland Today," *The Bell*, XVI (April, 1948), 40.

23. "Colored Balloons," pp. 12 and 21.

24. Sean O'Faolain's "Colored Balloons—a Letter" (*The Bell*, XV [January, 1948], 61 - 62) is typical of the responses that Kavanagh's plea provoked.

25. P. 36.

26. P. 84.

27. "Maurice Walsh's New Novel," *Irish Times*, July 20, 1940, p. 5.

28. "Auden and the Creative Mind," 33.

29. P. 66.

30. See "Round the Cinemas," February 22, 1946, p. 5; March 28, 1947, p. 7; March 22, 1946, p. 5; and June 28, 1946, p. 5.

31. "Letter from Ireland," LXXIV (August, 1949), 286.

32. "Diary," September, 1950, p. 85.

33. "A World of Praise," September 19, 1942, p. 2.

34. This poem and "From Failure Up," though written during Kavanagh's middle period, were not included in *A Soul for Sale*.

35. "War and Love," January 28, 1949, p. 3.

Chapter Five

1. "Note Book," National Library of Ireland Ms. 3218 [entry dated: June 11, 1924], p. 15.

2. "Round the Cinemas," March 22, 1946, p. 5.

3. *November Haggard*, ed. Peter Kavanagh (New York, 1971), p. 72.

4. Ibid., pp. 73 - 74.

5. Ibid., p. 15.

6. See, e.g., "The Poetic Spirit," *Creation*, I (August, 1957), 49.

7. "Poets on Poetry," *X*, I (March, 1960), 156.

8. "A Poem Gives Back My Youth," *Irish Farmers' Journal*, May 30, 1959, p. 22.

9. *Self Portrait*, p. 25.

10. In addition to John Montague's review, "Isolation and Cunning: Recent Irish Verse," *Poetry*, LXXXXII (July 4, 1959), and Douglas Sealy's article, "The Writings of Patrick Kavanagh," *The Dublin Magazine*, IV (Autumn-Winter, 1965), see Anthony Cronin, "Innocence and Experience: The Poetry of Patrick Kavanagh," *Nimbus*, III (Winter, 1956); John Hewitt, "The Cobbler's Song," *Threshold*, V (Spring, 1961); John Jordan, "Mr. Kavanagh's Progress," *Studies*, XXXXIX (Fall, 1960); John Rees Moore, "Now Yeats Has Gone: Three Irish Poets," *The Hollins Critic*, II (1966); Robin Skelton, "Life at Work," *Poetry*, CVI (June, 1965); and David Wright, "Patrick Kavanagh: 1905 - 1967," *London Magazine*, VIII (April, 1968).

11. See, e.g., *November Haggard*, pp. 75 - 76 and "The Gallivanting Poet," 63 - 70.

12. *November Haggard*, p. 2.

13. *Lapped Furrows*, pp. 202 - 203.

14. "From Monaghan to the Grand Canal," 34.

15. *November Haggard*, p. 73.

16. Ibid., p. 65.

17. Titled "News Item" in *Collected Poems*.

18. *Poet's Choice*, ed. Paul Engle and Joseph Langland (New York, 1966), p. 66.

19. "From Monaghan to the Grand Canal," 34.

20. See, e.g., Hayden Carruth, "Problems of Maturity," *Poetry*, CI (December, 1962), and Douglas Sealy, "The Writings of Patrick Kavanagh."

Chapter Six

1. See "Thank You, Thank You" in *Collected Poems*, pp. 192 - 93.

2. "Author's Note" opens with this statement: "I have never been much considered by the English critics" (p. xiii).

3. See, e.g., Robert Farren, "The Irish Number of *Horizon*," *Irish Times*, February 21, 1942, p. 5.

4. See, e.g., Richard Weber, "The Poetry of Patrick Kavanagh," *Icarus*, VI (May, 1956), 22 - 26.

5. See, e.g., James Liddy, *Homage to Patrick Kavanagh*, Versheet 3, New Writers Press, Dublin, 1971; Donald Torchiana, "Some Dublin Afterthoughts," *Tri-Quarterly Review*, IV (Autumn, 1965), 140 - 45; Sean Cronin, "Baggot Street Bard," *Commonweal*, January 12, 1968, pp. 447 - 48; and Paul Potts, "Patrick Kavanagh, the Poems and the Poet," *London Magazine*, February 2, 1963, pp. 78 - 81.

6. A representative list of Kavanaghisms is presented on pp. 25 - 30 of *Collected Pruse*.

7. *Lapped Furrows*, p. 116.

8. *November Haggard*, pp. 24 - 30.

9. *Lapped Furrows*, p. 114.

10. *November Haggard*, p. 60.

11. "Poetry Is Not Really an Art," May, 1964, p. 16.

12. *Collected Pruse*, p. 192.

13. *Lapped Furrows*, p. 250.

Selected Bibliography

PRIMARY SOURCES

1. Poetry
Ploughman and Other Poems. London: Macmillan and Co., Ltd., 1936.
The Great Hunger. Dublin: The Cuala Hand Press, 1942.
A Soul for Sale. London: Macmillan and Co., Ltd., 1947.
Recent Poems. New York: The Peter Kavanagh Hand Press, 1958.
Come Dance with Kitty Stobling and Other Poems. London: Longmans, Green and Co., Ltd., 1960.
Collected Poems. London: MacGibbon and Kee, Ltd., 1964.
The Complete Poems of Patrick Kavanagh. New York: The Peter Kavanagh Hand Press, 1972.

2. Fiction
"Three Glimpses of Life." *The Bell*, VIII (July, 1944).
"The Cobbler and the Football Team." *The Irish Press*, March 6, 1946.
"Stars in Muddy Puddles." *The Irish Press*, April 14, 1946.
"One Summer Evening in the Month of June." *The Irish Press*, June 15, 1946.
"Four Picturizations." *The Bell*, XIV (May, June, July, September, 1947).
"Feasts and Feasts." *The Standard*, April 4, 1947.
"The Good Child." *The Standard*, December 24, 1947.
Tarry Flynn. London: The Pilot Press, Ltd., 1948.
"Three Pieces from a Novel." *The Bell*, XVII (August, 1951).
"Pages from a Literary Novel." *The Bell* XIX (February, 1954).
By Night Unstarred. Dublin: Goldsmith Press, Ltd., 1977.

3. Autobiography
"Childhood of an Irishman." *Nineteenth Century*, October & December, 1937.
The Green Fool. London: Michael Joseph, Ltd., 1938.
Self Portrait. Dublin: The Dolmen Press, Ltd., 1964.

4. Prose
Collected Pruse. London: MacGibbon and Kee, Ltd., 1967.
November Haggard. New York: The Peter Kavanagh Hand Press, 1972.

Articles/Essays Not Reprinted in Collections:

"Patrick Kavanagh Goes to Knock." *The Standard*, May 8, 1942.
"When You Go to Lough Derg." *The Standard*, June 12, 1942.
"The Church and the Poets." *The Standard*, July 3, 1942.
"The Playboy of the Western World." *The Standard*, September 18, 1942.
"Eithical Standards." *The Standard*, April 2, 1943.
"Art Is Workshop." *The Standard*, April 23, 1943.
"Two Sides of the Picture." *The Standard*, April 30, 1943.
"The Road to Nowhere." *The Standard*, May 14, 1943.
"The Anglo-Irish Mind." *The Standard*, May 28, 1943.
"Critics, Critics, Critics." *The Standard*, June 11, 1943.
"The Tailor and Ansty." *Irish Times*, September 18, 1943.
"William Carleton." *Irish Times*, January 13, 1945.
"A Strange Irish Poet." *Irish Times*, March 30, 1945.
"I Saw Some Gay Strangers." *The Irish Press*, July 7, 1945.
"Man of Croagh Patrick." *The Standard*, August 3, 1945.
"Peasantry with a Meaning." *The Standard*, August 24, 1945.
"Davis Says to Me." *The Standard*, August 31, 1945.
"Fifty Years Achievement." *The Standard*, September 7, 1945.
"Sunday in the Country." *The Standard*, October 5, 1945.
"A Conversation with Memory." *The Standard*, December 7, 1945.
"The Seed of Poetry." *The Standard*, Easter, 1948.
"Poetry in Ireland Today." *The Bell*, XVI (April, 1948).
"Letter from Ireland." *Poetry*, XXXVII (August, 1949).
"Old Wives Tales of Ireland." *The Family Doctor*, June, 1952.
"The Poetic Situation in America." *Irish Times*, June 6, 1957.
"The Poetic Spirit." *Creation*, I (August, 1957).
"Christmas in New York." *Creation*, I (December, 1957).
"The Death of Nationalism." *National Observer*, September, 1958.
"A Piece of Nonsense." *Irish Farmers' Journal*, October 4, 1958.
"A World of Sensibility." *Irish Mythology: A Dictionary*. New York: The
    Peter Kavanagh Hand Press, 1959.
"On a Column." *National Observer*, July, 1959.
"The King is Not in Residence." *National Observer*, August, 1959.
"Roger Casement." *National Observer*, September, 1959.
"In Praise of Wells." *Ireland of the Welcomes*, September-October, 1959.
"The Television Monster." *National Observer*, October, 1959.
"The Do Gooders." *National Observer*, November, 1959.
"Art for Ballydehob." *National Observer*, January, 1960.
"Poets on Poetry." *X*, I (March, 1960).
"George Moore's Yeats." *Irish Times*, June 10, 1965.

5.   Serial Publications

"City Commentary," under "Piers Plowman." *The Irish Press*, September
    14, 1942 to February 8, 1944.

"Literary Scene." *The Standard,* February 26, 1943 to June 11, 1943.
"Round the Cinemas." *The Standard,* February 22, 1946 to July 8, 1949.
"Diary." *Envoy,* December, 1949 to July, 1951.
Kavanagh's Weekly, April 12, 1952 to July 5, 1952.
A monthly column. *Creation,* June, 1957 to December, 1957.
A weekly column. *Irish Farmers' Journal,* June 14, 1958 to March 9, 1963.
"A Column." *National Observer,* July, 1959 to January, 1960.
A weekly column. *RTV Guide,* January 17, 1964 to October 7, 1966.

6. Letters
Lapped Furrows. New York: The Peter Kavanagh Hand Press, 1969.

7. Manuscripts
"Account Book of James Kavanagh 1911 to 1929." National Library of
    Ireland Ms. 3220.
"Notebook." National Library of Ireland Ms. 3218.
"The Green Fool." National Library of Ireland Ms. 3213 - 3214.
"Cobblers Account Book." National Library of Ireland Ms. 3217.
"The Great Hunger." National Library of Ireland Ms. 3216.
"The Seed and the Soil" and "For Anna Quinn" (poems). National Library
    of Ireland Ms. 9579.

8. Recordings
"The Great Hunger." Tape recording of portions from the poem. Harvard
    University, 1947.
"Poems and Lectures." Tape recording of miscellaneous materials in-
    cluding reading given at Poetry International, London, 1967. Trinity
    College, Dublin, 1972.
"A Reading at Poetry International, London, 1967." Tape recording.
    University of Chicago, 1967.
Almost Everything: Written and Spoken by Patrick Kavanagh. Claddagh
    Records, Ltd., October 16, 1963.

9. Broadcasts
Radio:
Radio Eireann: "A Reading," February 20, 1936,
"Discussion," April 21, 1938.
"Literary Conversation: F. R. Higgins, Patrick Kavanagh and Louis
    MacNeice," October 12, 1939.
"Country Commentary," December 27, 1939.
"As I Roved Out," January 3, 11, 17, 1940.
"Looking Back," September 14, 1941.
"A Goat Tethered Outside the Bailey," February 2, 1953.
"This is No Book," September 17, 1953.
"The Gambler," September 23, 1953.
"Return in Harvest," October 10, 1953.

"My Country Christmas," December 24, 1953.
"A Hospital Notebook," September 4, 1955.
BBC Northern Ireland: "County Down," October 20, 1938.
BBC Welsh Region: "Nationalism in Literature," March 22, 1963.
BBC Third Program, London: "Thinking of Other Things," February 20, 1951.
"Carleton and Irishness," July 30, 1951.
"Introduction to a Reading of *The Great Hunger*," May 13, 1960.
"New Comment Series" (with Peter Duval-Smith), September 18, 1964.
Television:
Radio Telefis Eireann: "Self Portrait," October 30, 1962.
"Image," October 12, 1964.

10.   Interviews
"Meet Mr. Patrick Kavanagh." *The Bell*, XVI (April, 1948).
"A Poet Goes Home." *The Sunday Press*, October 11, 1964.
"Poetry Is Not Really an Art." *Hibernia*, May, 1964.
"Kavanagh's America." *Hibernia*, July, 1966.

11.   Miscellaneous
The Journal of Irish Literature: A Patrick Kavanagh Number. ed. John Nemo, VI (January, 1977).

SECONDARY SOURCES

1.   Anonymous News Items and Reviews
"Epitaph to a Poet." *The Irish Press*, August 21, 1968, p. 8. Short sketch in praise of Kavanagh's poetic achievement.
"Notes and Comments." *New Yorker*, December 9, 1967, pp. 51 - 52. Notice of Kavanagh's death.
"Profile: Patrick Kavanagh." *The Leader*, October 11, 1952, pp. 8 - 12. The famous (or infamous, depending on one's point of view) sketch that occasioned the fateful libel action. The attempt is to savage Kavanagh by employing his own critical methods.
Time, December 8, 1967, p. 108. Death notice with brief evaluative comment.

2.   Other Secondary Sources
BARDWELL, LELAND. "Poetry in the Sixties." *Dublin Arts Festival '70.* Official Program. Hails Kavanagh as chief influence on younger Irish poets.
BOLAND, EAVAN; SEAMUS HEANEY; MICHAEL HARTNETT; and LIAM MILLER. "The Future of Irish Poetry: A Discussion." *Irish Times*, February 5, 1970, p. 14. Considerable discussion of Kavanagh's positive influence on the development of recent Irish poetry. *The Great Hunger* is praised as a watershed for new Irish writers.

BRACKEN, T. "Patrick Kavanagh." *The Evening Herald*, December 7, 1967, p. 9. Unrewarding eulogy.

BRADY, PHELIM. "Profile: Patrick Kavanagh." *Empire News*, October 14, 1951, p. 15. The intention is to provide a provocative piece on Kavanagh's eccentricities, but what is delivered is an unrewarding rerun of Kavanagh's remarks as set down in *The Bell* interview.

BUTLER, HUBERT. "*Envoy* and Mr. Kavanagh." *The Bell*, XVII (September, 1951), 32 - 41. Interesting assessment of Kavanagh's monthly contribution to *Envoy*. Demonstrates the frequent faults in Kavanagh's critical pronouncements. Definitely worth reading.

CHILDS, SISTER MARYANNA. "P. K.: a Green Memory." *Catholic World*, March, 1968, pp. 269 - 70. Brief biographical sketch praising Kavanagh's work as a whole and placing him in the forefront of Irish writers.

COLUM, PADRAIC. "A Note on P. K." *The Kilkenny Magazine*, IV (Summer, 1962), 33 - 36. Examines relationship to the post-Celtic Revival period.

CRONIN, ANTHONY. "Innocence and Experience: the Poetry of Patrick Kavanagh." *Nimbus*, III (Winter, 1956), 20 - 23. A general survey of Kavangh's literary career by one of his followers.

CRONIN, SEAN. "Baggot Street Bard." *Commonweal*, January 12, 1968, pp. 447 - 48. A eulogy commenting on Kavanagh's Dublin haunts, his general literary themes, and his personality.

FREYER, GRATTAN. "Patrick Kavanagh." *Eire-Ireland*, III (Winter, 1968), 17 - 23. A general survey of Kavanagh's entire literary career which evaluates his principal works and attempts to place him in the middle Irish writing since 1940.

GERARD, PAUL. "Poetry in Ireland: 1930 - 1950." *Envoy*, VIII (July, 1950), 65 - 74. Useful sketch of the poetic developments in Ireland during the period Kavanagh came to the forefront. Kavanagh is one of a number of Irish poets treated.

HEWITT, JOHN. "The Cobbler's Song: a Consideration of the Work of Patrick Kavanagh." *Threshold*, V (Spring, 1961), 42 - 51. Balanced examination of Kavanagh's progress from *Ploughman and Other Poems* to *Come Dance with Kitty Stobling*. Emphasis is on later poems.

JORDAN, JOHN. "A Few Thoughts about Patrick Kavanagh." *Poetry Ireland*, IV (Summer, 1964), 123 - 26. An interesting essay on the compilation and arrangement of *Collected Poems*, with brief comments on Kavanagh's poetic development.

————. "Mr. Kavanagh's Progress." *Studies*, XXXXIX (Fall, 1960), 295 - 304. Examines Kavanagh's poetry of the 1950s in depth, with general background on his earlier writing.

KAVANAGH, PETER. "My Wild Irish Weekly." *American Mercury*, September, 1952, pp. 87 - 91. Interesting though somewhat prejudiced account of the rise and fall of *Kavanagh's Weekly*.

————. *The Garden of the Golden Apples*. New York: The Peter Kavanagh Hand Press, 1972. A very useful and thorough bibliography of

Kavanagh materials. Unfortunately, it was printed in a very limited edition and is difficult to obtain.

KENNELLY, BRENDAN. "Markings: Patrick Kavanagh." *RTV Guide*, November 26, 1966, pp. 8 - 9. Offers praise for Kavanagh's contributions to Irish literature.

————. "Patrick Kavanagh." *Ariel*, I (July, 1970), 7 - 28. Focus on Kavanagh's ideas about comedy as a philosophy for literature. Traces and evaluates Kavanagh's development as a poet. One of the more useful and knowledgeable pieces on the poet.

MCLAUGHLIN, THOMAS. "Patrick Kavanagh and the 'Ireland Myth.' " *The Honest Ulsterman*, May 13, 1969, pp. 41 - 44. Argues that Kavanagh stood above national writers, that he was a "world class" poet.

MCMAHON, SEAN. "The Parish and the Universe: a Consideration of *Tarry Flynn*." *Eire-Ireland*, III (Autumn, 1968), 157 - 169. Praises the novel and presents a strong case for its being ranked one of the best realistic novels of Irish rural life.

MERCIER, VIVIAN. "The Arts in Ireland." *Commonweal*, June 6, 1947, pp. 183 - 85. Survey of Irish literary matters after the war. Kavanagh is one of a number of writers mentioned. Useful background data.

NEMO, JOHN. "A Bibliography of Materials by and about Patrick Kavanagh." *Irish University Review*, III (Spring, 1973), 80 - 106. Compiled before *Garden of the Golden Apples*, this article presents a thorough list of both primary and secondary sources, together with a publishing history of the poetry.

————. "A Joust with the Philistines: Patrick Kavanagh's Cultural Criticism." *The Journal of Irish Literature*, IV (May, 1975), 65 - 75. Evaluates Kavanagh's contribution and influence in the area of Irish cultural criticism.

————. "The Green Knight: Patrick Kavanagh's Venture into Criticism." *Studies*, LXIII (Autumn, 1974), 282 - 94. Traces Kavanagh's practice of literary criticism from the late 1930s to the 1960s.

NEWTON, J. M. "Patrick Kavanagh's Imagination." *Delta*, XXXVII (Autumn, 1965), 4 - 8. Essentially a summary of the ideas that unify *Collected Poems*.

O'BRIEN, DARCY. *Patrick Kavanagh*. Lewisburg: Bucknell University Press, 1975. Monograph examining the stages of Kavanagh's literary development.

O'KEEFFE, TIMOTHY. "God Is Good to Patrick Kavanagh." *Two Rivers*, I (Spring, 1970), 71 - 74. Presenting the story behind the correspondence between Patrick and Peter Kavanagh which is published under the title, *Lapped Furrows*.

PAYNE, BASIL. "The Poetry of Patrick Kavanagh." *Studies*, XXXXIX (Fall, 1960), 279 - 94. Excellent study of Kavanagh's poetic development, with particular attention to poetry of the 1940s.

PLUNKETT, JAMES. "Pulled Weeds on the Ridge." *The Bell*, XVII (March, 1952), 69 - 78. Thorough analysis of *The Great Hunger*.

POTTS, PAUL. "In Retrospect: Patrick Kavanagh." *Twentieth Century*, CLXXVII (Spring, 1968), 48 - 51. Recollection of Kavanagh's literary career by one of his ardent admirers. Very subjective.

————. "Patrick Kavanagh, the Poems and the Poet." *London Magazine*, February 2, 1963, pp. 78 - 81. Presents a good example of the poetry being judged on the basis of the poet's personality.

ROSENTHAL, M. L. *The New Poets*. New York: Oxford University Press, 1967, pp. 275 - 83. Portion of a chapter devoted to Irish poets since World War II. Treats Kavanagh as a rural lyricist.

RYAN, JOHN. "Editorial." *The Dublin Magazine*, VI (Spring, 1968), 3 - 5. Discusses central themes in Kavanagh's writing. Speaks in particular to his rural realism.

SEALY, DOUGLAS. "The Writings of Patrick Kavanagh." *The Dublin Magazine*, III (Winter, 1965), 5 - 23. General summary statement of Kavanagh's literary development. Interesting comments on *Envoy* materials. Very critical of Kavanagh's thinking and disorganized criticism.

SHEEDY, LARRY. "How Kavanagh Told His Story." *Irish Farmers' Journal*, August 18, 1962. Background information on the characters and locality of *Tarry Flynn*.

SISSMAN, L. E. "Patrick Kavanagh, an Annotated Exequy." *New Yorker*, XXXXIV (May 4, 1968), 51. List of eulogies.

TORCHIANA, DONALD. "Some Dublin Afterthoughts." *Tri-Quarterly Review*, IV (Autumn, 1965), 140 - 145. Review of Kavanagh's appearance at Northwestern University, Chicago.

WARNER, ALAN. *Clay Is the Word*. Dublin: The Dolmen Press, 1973. Chapters on Kavanagh's criticism, his rural background, and his subjects and themes. Fails to penetrate the surface of the poetry.

WEBER, RICHARD. "The Poetry of Patrick Kavanagh." *Icarus*, VI (May, 1956), 22 - 25. General essay on a variety of items, themes, subjects, and technique.

WHITE, J. "Kavanagh Case." *Spectator*, March 5, 1954, pp. 254 - 56. Offers comments and summary of the libel action against *The Leader*.

WRIGHT, DAVID. "Patrick Kavanagh: 1905 - 1967." *London Magazine*, VIII (April, 1968), 22 - 29. Attempts to trace the development of Kavanagh's ideas about literature and the growth of his poetic talent.

Index

(The works of Kavanagh are listed under his name)